FACILITATION

A door to creative leadership
4th edition

Blair Miller   Jonathan Vehar   Roger Firestien   Sarah Thurber   Dorte Nielsen

CREATIVE PROCESS *series*: Part 2

FACILITATION
a door to creative leadership

Blair Miller
Jonathan Vehar
Roger Firestien
Sarah Thurber
Dorte Nielsen

4th edition, © 2011

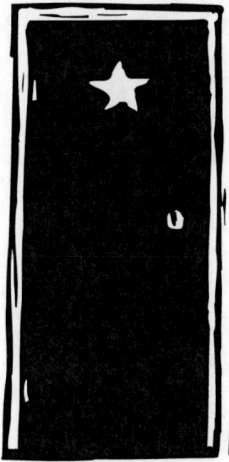

For more information about training materials in creativity, innovation and problem solving, please contact: FourSight, LLC. www.foursightonline.com

© 2011 Blair Miller, Jonathan Vehar, Roger Firestien, Sarah Thurber & Dorte Nielsen. All rights reserved. No portion of this publication may be reproduced, stored in a retrieval system or transmitted in any form or by any means, electronic, mechanical, photocopying, recording or otherwise, without the prior written permission of the publisher. Printed in the United States of America.

Published by FourSight, LLC, 1809 Central Street, Evanston, IL 60201 USA

FACILITATION

Table of Contents

Welcome! 4
Getting Started 5
The Goal 6

Facilitation Basics 7
Process v. Content 8
Roles in a CPS Session 9
The CPS Facilitator 10
The Client 11
The Resource Group 12
Facts on CPS Facilitators 13
Types of CPS Facilitation 14
Guidelines for Facilitators 15

Preparing for the Session 17
Meeting the Client 18
During the Meeting 19
Gather Ye Data 20
Is CPS a Good Fit? 21
A CPS Diagnosis 22
Client Interview Worksheet 23
Coaching Your Client 24
Posters to Prepare 25
Equipment & Logistics 28
Ideal Room Set Up 29
CPS Facilitator Feedback Form 30

Facilitating the Session 31
Opening the Session 32
Suggestions for Working Together ... 33
Jump Starting the Session 34
Warm-Up Exercises 35
Creative Questioning 36
Wait Time 37
Closing the Session 38
Stages of Group Development 40
Team Effectiveness 41
Group Size 42

FACILITATION

Using the CPS Process 43
The FourSight Model 45
The Expert Model 46
The Executive Step 47
Assess the Situation 48
Explore the Vision 50
Formulate the Challenge 52
Explore Ideas 54
Formulate Solutions 56
Explore Acceptance 58
Formulate Action Plan 60
Thinking Skills 62
Affective Skills 63
CPS Toolbox—Diverge 64
CPS Toolbox—Converge 65
Facilitator Cheat Sheet 66

Advanced Facilitation Tips 69
Facilitator All-Star Tips 70
Facilitator as Hero 72
Facilitator Speak 76
Selecting a Resource Group 78

Appendix 81
CPS Facilitator Self Assessment 83
Worksheets 87
To Learn More 102
References 103

Acknowledgments
The authors want to acknowledge the individuals and organizations who were indispensible in creating this book:

International Center for Studies in Creativity
Creative Education Foundation
Linda L. Avarello
John Cabra
Dennis Carter
Sue Ellen Coleman
Hedria P. Lunken
Gerard J. Puccio
Russell Schoen

© 2011 Miller, Vehar, Firestien, Thurber, Nielsen

FACILITATION

Welcome!

Dear Creative Leader,

Get ready for a fun, interactive learning experience, full of implications—and applications—for your personal and professional life. You will walk away from this facilitator training course with skills, tools and information that are tremendously practical and strategically useful in business, and in life.

As we embark on this study of Creative Problem Solving (CPS) facilitation, keep in mind that the authors of this book didn't make this business up. We are, in fact, standing on the shoulders of giants: academic researchers, corporate managers and other creative geniuses who have painstakingly studied styles of problem solving and leadership over the course of 50 years to arrive at what we now know as CPS facilitation.

Thanks to the efforts of Creative Problem Solving pioneers like Alex Osborn and Sid Parnes, plus pioneering organizations like the International Center for Studies in Creativity and the Creative Education Foundation, the road we are about to walk has become a newly paved path to creative leadership. If you pursue the art of leadership, you will find that facilitation is as profound a skill as you make it: You can use it to run a meeting, or change an entire corporate culture. Even for first-timers, CPS facilitation will help you promote creativity, innovation and team initiative in your organization.

Throughout this book you will find scattered quotes, offering insights into leadership, creativity, inspiration and facilitation. Some names you will recognize. Others are words of wisdom from contemporary facilitators, working hard to perfect their craft.

> "Facilitation is a journey, not a destination. You are a better facilitator today than you were yesterday, but not half the facilitator you will be tomorrow."
>
> BILL SHEPHARD

Welcome along on this journey of discovery.

Blair Miller
Jonathan Vehar
Roger Firestien
Sarah Thurber
Dorte Nielsen

Bon Voyage!

FACILITATION

Getting Started

A Few Prerequisites
Welcome to "Facilitation: A Door to Creative Leadership." Before we plunge into this book, there are a few concepts you should already have under your belt.

Creative Problem Solving
The first one is factual: You should be familiar with Creative Problem Solving (CPS)—the process and the vocabulary. If you've participated in a CPS training session, that's a good start. Don't worry if all the terms and tools aren't fresh in your head, we'll have charts and handouts to remind you along the way.

Deferred Judgment
The second thing you should know is more "behavioral" in nature: It's the theory and practice of deferred judgment—the cornerstone of creative leadership.
Unlike the traditional manager who
responds to ideas with critical judgment, saying "Right!" "Wrong!" "Good idea!" "Bad idea!" the facilitator uses deferred judgment with the goal of eliciting more and better ideas. The facilitator responds to ideas, saying "Great! Now build on that." "What else does that idea make you think of?" "What could we do to overcome any possible barriers to that idea?" Deferred judgment gives young ideas breathing room to grow and improve. It is a fundamental behavior of great facilitators—and creative leaders.

Do not drop this on an idea.

FACILITATION

Vrooom....

"You think you have a limit... As soon as you touch this limit, something happens to you; suddenly you can go a little bit further. With your mind power, your determination, your instinct and your experience..., you can fly very high."

— Aryton Senna
World Champion
Race Car Driver

The Goal

A Personal Breakthrough

This book will train you to help others solve problems and meet challenges. But the primary beneficiary is you!

The tools and concepts you are about to study are challenging. They require practice and a commitment. As you become an increasingly skilled facilitator, you will empower people to solve their own problems, not provide them with solutions. Leading groups to their own breakthroughs is extremely rewarding work—for your organization, for your clients and for you.

What you'll accomplish:

- *improve and expand communication skills*
- *examine links between creativity and leadership*
- *practice group management skills*
- *practice effective presentation skills*
- *study the implications of group dynamics on CPS facilitation*
- *learn to conduct a client interview*
- *facilitate a CPS session and get coaching and feedback*
- *develop a plan of action for a personal or professional challenge*

FACILITATION

Facilitation Basics

> "You cannot be a leader and ask other people to follow you, unless you know how to follow, too."
>
> SAM RAYBURN

The intriguing thing about Creative Problem Solving (CPS) is that it can help solve nearly ANY type of problem: from improving sales to improving marriages, from writing a mission statement to deploying a mission.

The reason CPS works on such a broad variety of problems is that it doesn't provide answers. It provides a sure-fire method of getting to answers. In CPS lingo, that means CPS handles "process" not "content." To solve problems consistently, both process and content are critical.

In facilitation ...

Process =
A sequence of actions or events (i.e. how something gets done.)

Content =
Facts, information or decisions about a specific issue (i.e. what gets done).

Process v. Content

© 2011 Miller, Vehar, Firestien, Thurber, Nielsen

FACILITATION

Process v. Content

The difference between how and what

Contrary to popular belief, *Process v. Content* is not a Supreme Court case that guarantees your right to be creative (that's in the Constitution). Process and content are the two distinct categories that cover everything involved with Creative Problem Solving. Think of process as *how* to solve the problem and content as *what* is the problem.

Process:
Process includes whatever steps, tools and techniques are used to facilitate a session. Process is the domain of the facilitator. A master facilitator uses process to direct the group so the client's needs are met. The facilitator is constantly making "process" decisions, such as: Should the group use brainstorming? What statement starters are appropriate? What techniques should the group use to converge? How can we best achieve the desired outcome? How should we close the meeting?

Content:
Content refers to the subject matter—all the facts, figures and data surrounding the problem. During the session, the client and resource group diverge on these content issues to come up with many options for the client, who then converges to narrow those options to a select few. The client "owns" the content, meaning the client makes the following content-driven decisions: Do we have enough ideas? Do we need to further refine the idea? What needs to happen next in the meeting?

Striking the balance
The interaction of process and content is the dance led by the facilitator. By managing the process, the facilitator allows the group to explore every aspect of the content with confidence that the client will achieve his or her goal. The brilliant ideas that come from the session fall into the category of content, but they result from the skillful use of process.

FACILITATION

Roles in a CPS Session

Separating Content from Process

There are several roles in a CPS session specifically designed to keep content and process distinct, so that both can make their maximum contribution.

Facilitator
The facilitator is the "process expert": the person (or team of people) responsible for monitoring and directing group process. The facilitator makes CPS process decisions based on the client's input.

Client
The client—whether an individual or group—is the primary owner of content (i.e. the challenge being explored). The client is responsible for sharing background information, generating ideas with the resource group and selecting ideas that best address the challenge.

Resource Group
The resource group supports the client by providing ideas, energy, insight and fresh perspectives to the CPS session.

Process Buddy
An assistant facilitator who helps out during the session to manage logistics and tasks so the lead facilitator can focus on the group.

> "Two of the most important things [for a facilitator] to remember are: Stay out of the content, and stay in the process."
>
> HEDRIA LUNKEN

The outcome of a CPS session on "H2 build a better mousetrap" will depend on whether your client is a homeowner... or a mouse.

FACILITATION

Facilitators: "Be a guide by the side, not a sage on the stage."

RUTH NOLLER

The CPS Facilitator

The "Process Expert"

The facilitator manages and monitors the problem-solving process. The facilitator is the "process expert."

In addition, facilitators ...

- Establish a supportive environment
- Are interested in others
- Are confident and flexible
- Remain affirmative and objective

"Good" CPS Facilitators

Do's ...	Don'ts ...
Develop a flexible process plan	Don't simply record the progress
Act as the process expert	Don't pose as the content expert
Serve as a process guide	Don't serve as the group leader
Stay out of content	Don't act as the primary decision maker
Reinforce CPS roles and guidelines and encourage participation	Don't take a passive role

© 2011 Miller, Vehar, Firestien, Thurber, Nielsen

FACILITATION

The Client
The "Owner" of the Challenge

The client determines the direction.
The client has decision-making authority.
The client provides background information.
The client is committed to solving the problem.

In addition, clients ...

- Are open-minded and flexible
- Contribute ideas and thoughts
- Give feedback to confirm the progress of the CPS session
- Have a positive outlook
- Model good listening and deferred judgment for the group

As a facilitator: "Listen to your client's needs, and use the process to support those needs."

GERARD PUCCIO

"Good" Clients

Do's ...	Don'ts ...
Value the input of others	Don't pretend to be the "know it all"
Focus on content	Don't act as a process expert
Own the challenge	Don't act simply as a representative
Be honest and give straight-forward answers	Don't operate based on hidden agendas
Come to the session well informed and prepared	Don't remain ambivalent about what the client wants

FACILITATION

The Resource Group

The "Idea Engine"

The resource group provides a wide range of ideas and viewpoints. The resource group is interested in the client's problem and works toward the client's goal.

In addition, resource groups ...

- Provide energy and enthusiasm
- Contribute to the flow of ideas
- Build on the ideas of others
- Understand the roles and act appropriately

"Being a resource group member can be exhausting. Give them a break every now and then. Working your resource group members to death is still a felony in many states."

JONATHAN VEHAR

"Good" Resource Groups

Do's ...	Don'ts ...
Offer unique backgrounds and viewpoints	*Don't attempt to be homogeneous*
Enthusiastically learn and use CPS	*Don't lack interest in CPS*
Commit to work for the client's goal	*Don't ignore the client's concern*
Provide lots of ideas or options	*Don't need to be experts on content*

Facts on CPS Facilitators

The Fiction
There are many misconceptions about what a facilitator does:

- Acts as flip chart secretary
- Paraphrases responses
- Solves problems by getting involved in content
- Leads discussions
- Motivates group
- Serves as scapegoat
- Offers administrative support
- Owns the problem

The Facts
But actually, a CPS facilitator:

- Manages the process
- Knows the process inside and out
- Stays out of content
- Is transparent to the outcome
- Is responsible to the client
- Ensures that the client's needs are met
- Keeps the group on track
- Makes sure logistics are handled

"Facilitation is rather like the art of improvisation. A good facilitator creates a safe and comfortable atmosphere and creates an illusion of balance. The balance is between structure and spontaneity, and discipline and freedom. A great facilitator can do all that from the top of a high wire."

Types of CPS Facilitation

Typically, a facilitator will work with a client and a resource group. It's also possible to facilitate the CPS process for a single client or even for yourself. Here are some pointers for each situation:

Facilitating for a Group

- The ideal resource group size is five to nine people.
- The facilitator acts solely as a process manager, leaving the resource group and client to focus on content.
- The facilitator guides the group, using tools and the CPS process.

Facilitating for One Client

- The facilitator's primary role here, again, is to guide the client, using the CPS process.
- If the client gets "stuck," the facilitator can contribute ideas and participate in content as well.
- Even here, don't push your ideas or opinions. Focus on giving the client what they need.

Facilitating Your Own Session

- When working on your own, you wear all three hats: facilitator, client and resource person.
- Try to alternate hats, keeping the process and the content separate in your mind.
- Use your knowledge of the CPS process to stay on track.

> "Your success is determined by the actions of the group and not by their recognition of your role in their success."
>
> DIANE FOUCAR-SZOCKI

Guidelines for Facilitators

Stay out of content.
Refrain from giving your ideas and opinions.

Keep it in their words.
Try to capture verbatim what the client and resource group members say. If it's too long to write, ask them to create a "headline" (newspaper style) that summarizes it.

Stay on track.
Use your knowledge of process to keep the client and resource group moving forward.

Deliver for the client.
Make sure the client gets what they need, not what you want or the group wants.

Pay attention.
Pay attention to the needs of the client and resource group. Be aware of the group's development and the relationship between members. Be prepared to resolve any developing issues.

Celebrate progress.
Make sure that the client and resource group understand what they've achieved.

Remember, the client knows best.
Keep your own opinions and biases out of the process. Don't lead or manipulate the group, no matter how right you think you are. The client knows their situation best.

FACILITATION

Notes:

FACILITATION

Preparing for the Session

"Plan diligently and be prepared to abandon your plan to meet the needs of the group and accomplish the desired outcome of the client."

BLAIR MILLER

There are some truly great facilitators. They help groups make astounding breakthroughs, while making their own role look almost effortless. These professionals are like the proverbial duck, who glides gracefully along the surface, but is paddling like mad under the water. The great facilitator is always thinking and always prepared. In fact, much of the real "work" of facilitation happens before you ever begin the CPS session. Here's how it looks under the surface.

My inner child is a duck.

FACILITATION

Meeting the Client

A Guide to Client Interviews

 **Facilitator and client—only.**
The client interview involves the facilitator and client only. This ensures privacy and confidentiality, as sensitive issues are often discussed.

 **Understand the client's needs.**
The facilitator should use this meeting to understand the specific challenge facing the client and to make sure that CPS is an appropriate way to address the challenge. By the end of the meeting the facilitator should be able to answer the following questions:

1) What is the key data around the challenge?
2) What is the statement of the challenge?
3) What CPS stage is an appropriate starting place for addressing the challenge?
4) What tools and techniques will be useful at the session?
5) What logistics must be covered?

The answers to these questions will help you plan the upcoming CPS session.

 **Somewhere comfortable and confidential.**
Any location for the meeting is appropriate as long as the client and facilitator can both talk candidly, comfortably and without unwanted interruption.

 **Give yourself some lead time.**
Try to schedule the client interview as far in advance as possible—several days or weeks before the actual facilitation. More planning time will allow the facilitator to anticipate needs and prepare for the session.

 **Be sure CPS is a good fit.**
Part of the facilitator's responsibility is to be sure CPS is appropriate for the challenge at hand. If not, be prepared to turn down the project or recommend another approach. (See page 21.)

FACILITATION

During the Meeting

How to Conduct a Client Interview

The client interview mirrors the Clarify step of CPS. During the discussion, the facilitator should work with the client to:

Explore the Vision

Find out about the client's initial concern, challenge or goal. You might lead the discussion by asking open-ended questions like, "Why are we here?" or "What do you hope to accomplish?" The answers will help you craft an initial statement of the challenge with the client.

Gather Data

Investigate the facts, feelings and issues that surround the challenge. Ask about the who, what, when, where and why of the situation. Find out what has been tried before. (For a complete list of questions, see the Client Interview Worksheet on page 23.) Review all this background data with the client, and select the key data to share with the resource group.

Formulate the Challenge

In the client interview, use tools for Clarifying to help pinpoint the challenge your client wants to address during the CPS session. Work with the client to craft some initial statements of the problem. (These could be goal, wish, challenge statements, problem statements, or action statements.)

Results of Client Session

The facilitator should now have the following:

- ☐ Information to complete the CPS Session Worksheet (page 23).
- ☐ Information to fill out flip charts that introduce the challenge to the resource group, (pages 25-27).
- ☐ An idea of who the resource group members will be.
- ☐ Confidence that the client understands the distinct roles (facilitator, client, resource group member) in a CPS session.
- ☐ Agreement with the client on the next steps required to make sure the CPS session takes place.

FACILITATION

Gather Ye Data
The facts are still a-flying

Good data can be elusive.

Dig for specific data
When gathering data during the client interview, go for specifics. Hard, fact-filled data gives the resource group a better springboard for developing quality problem statements and innovative solutions. Look for objective measures rather than subjective opinions. If you ask, "How long has this been a problem?" and the client answers, "A long time," keep probing. Ask, "Can you give me a sense of just how long? When specifically did it start?" Your genuine interest and curiosity will help the client open up with details. Perhaps even more valuable, unraveling the data can help a client clarify exactly what they do and don't know about a problem. An effective client interview can draw out critical information and help separate fact from opinion—a great start to any problem-solving session.

Prep specific data
When you prepare data for the resource group, continue to drive for details. Instead of listing your data as, "We don't have enough money," be more specific, "We need $20,000 to complete this project." Instead of saying, "I don't have enough time to finish this project," be more precise, "The project is due May 1." By avoiding generalities in the data, you give the resource group more to work with and increase the odds of hitting on great solutions.

Leverage the data/idea connection
When the client shares key data with the resource group at the beginning of the CPS session, encourage listeners to jot down ideas and make connections. Remind them to use the appropriate statement starters. For example, if the session begins in the Clarify stage, the resource group members can use "How to...," "How might...," "In what ways might..." or "What might be all the..." to generate problem statements during data sharing. If the session is in the Generate Ideas stage, they can write their ideas on post-it notes.

FACILITATION

Is CPS a Good Fit?

Check Ownership, Motivation, Imagination

Now that you've got all the relevant data, take a moment to confirm that CPS is appropriate for the challenge at hand. CPS is probably a good fit if you can answer "yes" to all of the following questions:

Ownership —
Does the client have the authority and accountability for this challenge? Is there agreement with the client's boss, staff, peers or customers that it is the client's responsibility to solve the problem?

Motivation —
Does the challenge require prompt attention? Does the client feel it's worth an investment of time and resources to address this challenge?

Imagination —
Is there a need for new thinking? Does the situation require imaginative, creative solutions?

Questions to test for ownership:

- Are you accountable for this task?

- Are you willing to be held accountable for accomplishing this goal—and suffer the consequences if you don't?

- Is this your problem to solve?

- Are other people counting on you to implement a solution to this problem?

- Do you own this challenge?

Does the client have a stake in it?

The importance of pinpointing "ownership" was initially explored by William Shephard, Roger Firestien and Diane Foucar-Szocki at Multiple Resource Associates and published in 1983 by Roger Firestien and Donald Treffinger and by Scott Isaksen.

FACILITATION

A CPS Diagnosis

Assessing the situation
The first step in creating a "process plan" for your CPS session

Once you have met with the client and determined that CPS is appropriate, you must decide where in the CPS process the session itself should begin. Use this basic diagnostic tool to help you.

If the situation is unclear or vague, and...
- you don't have all the facts
- there is no clear direction

... begin your CPS session in **Clarify**.

If a clearly defined problem already exists, but...
- there is no clear solution
- there is a need for a variety of ideas

... begin your CPS session in **Ideate**.

If good ideas must be strengthened and turned into workable solutions, and...
- you need to refine the ideas
- you need to work out the details

... begin your CPS session in **Develop**.

If your solution is clear, and...
- there is a need to gain acceptance and support
- a plan needs to be developed for implementation

... begin your CPS session in **Implement**.

FACILITATION

Client Interview Worksheet

Based on your client interview, complete the information below. Attach extra pages as needed, especially for "data."

Client : _____
Date: _____
Area of Concern (initial goal, wish, challenge): IWBGI.... I wish... _____
_____
_____

Data

What is a brief history of the situation?
Who is involved in the situation?
Who is the decision maker?
How do you own this challenge?
Who needs to be a part of the solution?
Who might gain if the situation is resolved?
What successes have you achieved so far?
What are things that have helped you?
What are some obstacles you've encountered?
Where have you found help? Obstacles?

When is the situation occurring or reoccurring?
When would you like to have action taken?
How long has this been a concern?
Why is it a concern for you?
Why might this be an opportunity for you?
What's been thought of or tried already?
What are your gut feelings about this challenge?
How are your feelings affecting your behavior?
What might be your ideal outcome or goal?
What else?

Initial problem statement(s): H2... HM... IWWM... WMBAT... _____
_____
_____

Purpose and desired outcomes of upcoming session:_____
_____
_____

Session Plan

CPS Stage: _____
Statement (w/starter):_____
Initial tool selection: _____
Session date: _____
Time: From _____ To _____
Location: _____
Logistical needs: _____

Resource group members: _____
_____

Who will begin session? _____
How? _____

General notes:

_____

© 2011 Miller, Vehar, Firestien, Thurber, Nielsen

FACILITATION

Coaching Your Client
How to help your client be great

Before the session, facilitators can encourage their clients to:

Come prepared to work.
Come prepared to really work for a solution. (The resource group will work hard, but they can't help you solve the problem without your participation.)

Listen generously.
Don't prematurely judge ideas.

Value novelty.
Be willing to try some new approaches.

Just say "yes..."
Furthermore, say "yes, and..." not "yes, but..."

Support the resource group.
Do not devalue the group's input (e.g. "I've already thought of that.")

Don't freak out.
If all else fails, call a time out.

Ask for what you need.
It's the client's responsibility to ensure they get what they want.

Offer honest input.
Be energetic in providing input. Be honest with the facilitator about the dynamics of the issue. Don't withhold vital information.

Choose your problem carefully.
Be sure you're working on something for which you want results.

Alert the facilitator to any changes.
Inform the facilitator of any change of heart or change in direction.

Have fun!
And don't forget to thank the resource group for their hard work.

FACILITATION

Posters to Prepare

Teaching Tools

The following pages show a series of flip chart posters that you can prepare before the CPS session. You will need your CPS Session Worksheet to complete the charts on page 26.

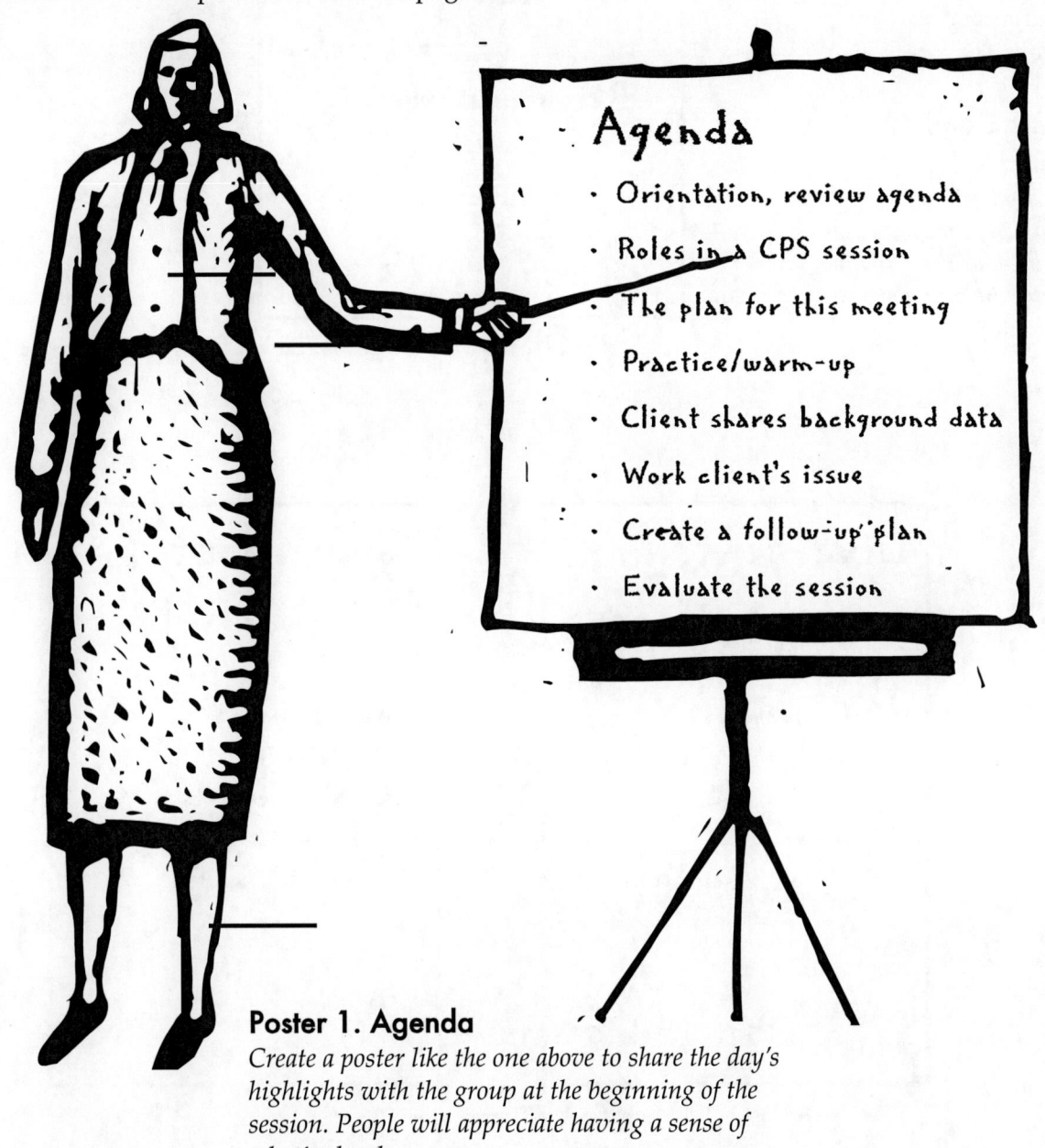

Poster 1. Agenda
Create a poster like the one above to share the day's highlights with the group at the beginning of the session. People will appreciate having a sense of what's ahead.

© 2011 Miller, Vehar, Firestien, Thurber, Nielsen

FACILITATION

Poster 2: CPS Roles...
Explain the different roles people will play during the CPS session. (For definitions, see page 9.) Clarifying this early will help the group keep "content" and "process" distinct and serve as an up front reminder that the client will ultimately make the decisions.

Posters 3 and 4: Ground Rules
The two charts below can be copied verbatim. They are the tried-and-true ground rules for diverging and converging.

1.
Roles in a CPS Session
- Client ----------------
- Facilitator ----------
- Resource Group

2.
Divergent Ground Rules
- Defer judgment
- Strive for quantity
- Seek wild and unusual ideas
- Build on other ideas

3.
Convergent Ground Rules
- Be affirmative
- Be deliberate
- Check objectives
- Improve ideas
- Consider novelty

FACILITATION

4. CLARIFY

> Statement of the goal, wish or challenge...IW, IWBGI
>
> Key Data:
> · data · data · data
> · data · data · data
> · data · data · data
> · data · data · data

Posters 4 - 6: *(pick one)*
Client Summary for the Resource Group
Depending on your CPS diagnosis, create one of the three flip charts on this page. If the session is going to start with Clarify, create chart 4 (on top). If you're starting with Ideating, use chart 5 (bottom left). If you're going to begin with Develop, use chart 6 (bottom right).

5. IDEATE

> Statement of the goal, wish or challenge...IW, IWBGI
>
> Key Data:
> · data · data · data · data
> · data · data · data · data
> · data · data · data · data
> · data · data · data · data
>
> Challenge statement...
> H2, HM, IWWM, WMBAT

6. DEVELOP

> Statement of the goal, wish or challenge...IW, IWBGI
>
> Key Data:
> · data · data   · data
> · data · data   · data
>
> Statement of the problem...
> H2, HM, IWWM, WMBAT
>
> What I see myself (us) doing is...

© 2011 Miller, Vehar, Firestien, Thurber, Nielsen

FACILITATION

Equipment & Logistics

Suggestions for a Facilitator's Kit

Timer
1 flip chart per group (with a stand and plenty of paper)
1 roll of masking tape for each flip chart
3"x 5" Post-it® pads for each participant
Colored dots
Colored magic markers
Sanford® Mr. Sketch Stix fine-tip markers
Vis-a-vis™ (overhead markers)
Pens / pencils
Chalk
Crayons
Extension cord and adapter
2 Flip charts w/stands and plenty of paper in front of room
Objects for Visual Connections

Equipment and Room Set-up

Area to hang completed flip chart papers
Overhead projector / screen (w/extra light bulb)
Compact disc or cassette player and music
Know the location of the nearest copy machine
Know the location of the nearest restrooms and fire exits
Drinking water

Ideal Room Set Up

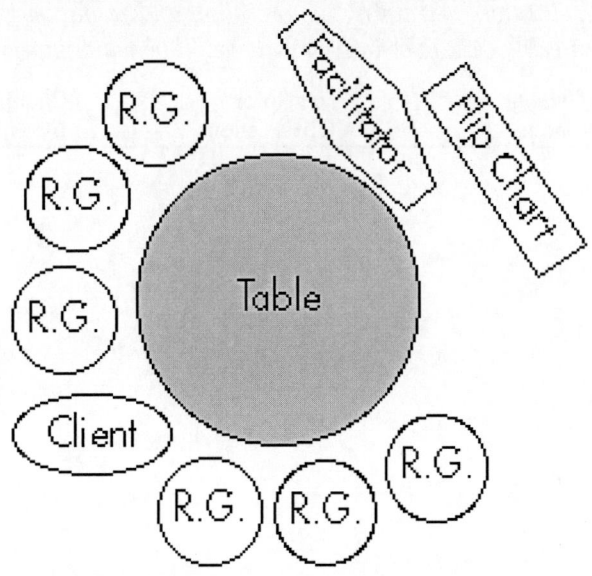
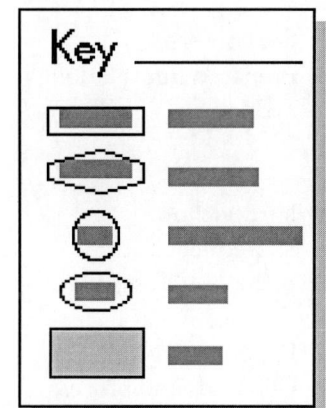

Other Options

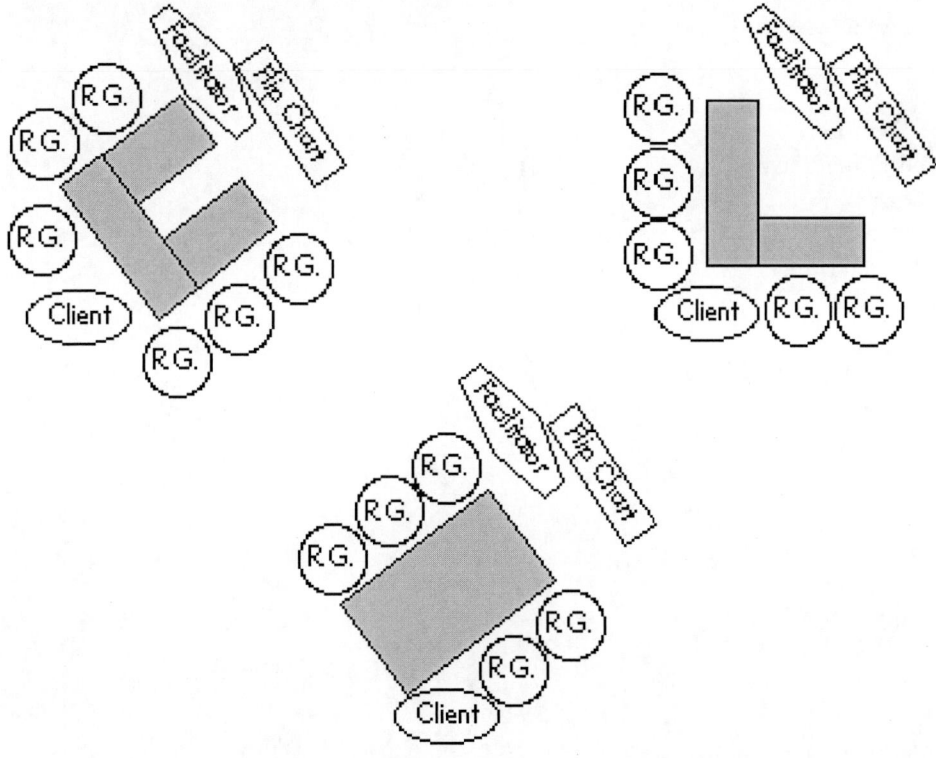

FACILITATION

FACILITATION

CPS Facilitator Feedback Form

Observation Guide

During the CPS session you will lead as a facilitator-in-training, your trainer and resource group will use this form to evaluate your performance. Look it over to see what they'll be watching for.

	Coach/Trainer Observations	Facilitator Observations	Client/Group Observations
☐ **Session Prep** Prepared information and logistics in advance			
☐ **Introduction** Shared focus and purpose of session			
☐ Explained agenda, CPS roles and process			
☐ Lead warm-up exercise; Reviewed divergent and convergent guidelines			
☐ Had client share output from client interview session			
☐ **During Session** Checked in regularly with client			
☐ Let client determine the direction			
☐ Selected appropriate divergent and convergent tools; Trained group in use of tools Tools used:			
☐ Transitioned between stages			
☐ **Closing** Identified next steps; Closed session			

FACILITATION

Facilitating the Session

A leader is best
When people barely know he exists.
Not so good
When people obey and acclaim him.
Worse when they despise him.
But of a good leader
Who talks little
When his work is done
His aim fulfilled
They will say
"We did it ourselves."

— Lao-Tsu

"A good facilitator trusts the group."

— Dee Young

A model for facilitation. Not.

FACILITATION

Opening the Session
Comfort • Etiquette • Confidentiality

> "Listening gives you the direction for which tools, techniques and process methodologies to use at a given moment."
>
> JOHN CABRA

Creature Comforts
Review with the group:

- Session schedule
- Breaks
- Restroom locations
- Refreshments (coffee, water, etc.)

Encourage people to take responsibility for their own personal comfort during the session.

Session Etiquette
Establish a few ground rules. Ask the group to:

- Show courtesy and respect by listening while the facilitator or other group members are addressing the group.
- Keep the focus on the client's needs.
- Reserve a separate pad of paper to write down any thoughts, comments or feelings they need to share with the group, and wait for an appropriate opportunity to bring them up.

Confidentiality
A critical reminder:

- Remember, this is a real client and a real challenge. Treat it with due respect.
- Speaking freely in the session requires discretion afterwards. All information, ideas and action plans shared during the session should remain confidential.

Suggestions for Working Together

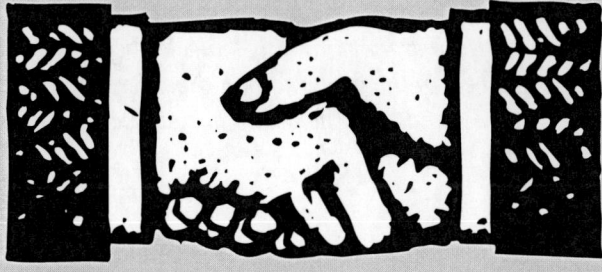

The following suggestions may sound simple, but when applied rigorously, they have helped ordinary groups achieve extraordinary results.

Act as friends
Treat each other with respect. Be supportive. Help others be successful.

Express yourself
Speak your mind in a way that people will be willing to listen.

Look for what's possible
Focus on the possibilities, not the obstacles.

Commit to learn
Be curious, be surprised, have your thinking provoked.

Challenge by choice
Take responsibility for your own safety. Encourage others with support, not pressure.

Acknowledge and appreciate
Take time to acknowledge the contributions of others and appreciate their greatness.

Listen generously
Try to suspend your own judgments, certainties and assumptions.

Be coachable
Be receptive to feedback and willing to change your thoughts, opinions and behaviors.

Have Fun
Enjoy yourself! Work hard and don't take yourself too seriously.

© 2011 Miller, Vehar, Firestien, Thurber, Nielsen

FACILITATION

Jump Start the Session

> "The greatest influence on a group's creative behavior is your behavior as a facilitator. Be a model for what you want the group to be."
>
> ROGER FIRESTIEN

Limbering up the Mind

Just as athletes need to stretch before a physical workout, CPS participants need to stretch their divergent thinking muscles before getting to work on the client's issue. Limber up the group with a divergent thinking exercise to raise the energy level and help the group achieve better, faster results (with less chance of injury).

Warm-up activities help groups:
- practice tools and techniques
- learn or review divergent ground rules
- get comfortable with working together
- set a climate to encourage laughter and exploration

Overcoming the "silly" factor

Most warm-up exercises are admittedly silly. They're designed that way on purpose. The subjects are common and non-threatening. Many of the ideas suggested will sound absurd or impractical. That's exactly the imaginative mindset the group needs when they eventually approach the "serious" problem. So don't let the "silly" factor deter you. If you sense resistance, explain the rationale for the warm-up exercise, and promise it will only take four minutes. That's all you need.

Some groups need an energy boost.

FACILITATION

Warm-Up Exercises

Go Ahead, Rack your Brain!
For each exercise you choose, set the goal of coming up with at least 30-50 ideas within three minutes. If the group doesn't reach the quota, keep pushing until they do.

In what ways might we improve...
List every conceivable way to improve:
- A bathtub
- A bicycle
- A stairway
- An automobile
- A telephone
- A glove
- Any other common object

How might you benefit from...
Your organization receives a generous gift from a benefactor, intended to benefit you financially. How might you benefit from the gift of:
- 1 million ping pong balls
- 100,000 left-handed gloves
- 10,000 broomsticks (sticks only, no brush attached)
- 500,000 defective computer disks

How might you use....
List every possible way you might use:
- A pencil
- A tire
- A brick
- A plunger

Many of the above warm-up exercises were developed and described in full by Sidney Parnes in *Creative Behavior Guidebook* and Donald Treffinger, Scott Isaksen and Roger Firestien in *Handbook for Creative Learning*. You can also practice using convergent techniques with these exercises after you generate lots of ideas.

FACILITATION

Creative Questioning

Divergent and Convergent questions

Creative Questioning
There are basically two types of questions to ask in a problem-solving session: divergent questions and convergent questions. Divergent questions call for many responses. They encourage more ideas. Convergent questions limit responses and can often be answered with a simple yes or no. Convergent questions are useful for closing down a group discussion or moving to another stage of the problem-solving process. Knowing when to ask the right type of question can greatly increase your effectiveness as a facilitator.

The following are some examples of
Divergent Questions:

What are all the uses you can possibly imagine for a brick?
What is every idea you can imagine for solving this problem?
What is your thinking?
Which restaurants could we go to for lunch?
In what ways can you make the lights burn in this experiment with a wire, switch and battery?
What else can you think of that will help us solve this problem?
Please tell me more about your idea.

The following are examples of
Convergent Questions:

Do you have any more ideas?
Do you like that color?
Will there be anything else?
Thanks, are there any other suggestions?
Do you like Chinese food?
Does your dog bite?

© 2011 Miller, Vehar, Firestien, Thurber, Nielsen

Wait Time

The power of the pause

Pauses during a facilitated session can be awkward, especially for the first-time facilitator. But as you gain more experience working with groups, you'll learn to distinguish between a pause that is dissipating creative energy and a pause that is pregnant with possibilities for a whole new wave of ideas.

For all the tap dancing you do as a facilitator to keep your group buzzing along, keep in mind that one simple but powerful technique to encourage group discussion is simply silence, or "wait time." Researcher Mary Budd-Rowe and her colleagues studied the questioning behavior of teachers and discovered that most teachers wait less than one second for students to reply to their questions. An analysis of student responses revealed that teachers with longer wait times—three seconds or more—generated more conversation, debate and increased speculative thinking by 700 percent!

Notice the big guy lets me do all the talking.

Wait time encourages creative thinking

Advice for facilitators: Although it may feel uncomfortable at first, increase your wait time after asking a question, and you will find that groups will participate more and generate more ideas. Wait time also allows group members who may be reluctant to participate an opening to get involved.

FACILITATION

Closing the Session
Creating a Follow-Up Plan

This may seem like an odd time to talk about wrapping up the session, but a strong finish to your CPS facilitation is a cornerstone to success. After all, if you haven't helped your client carry this facilitation effort forward, you haven't helped your client.

When you finish facilitating the CPS process, the meeting is not over. Some loose ends still need to be tied up to maximize the value of all the time and energy spent in the CPS session.

Review meeting objectives
Check with the client to make sure their objectives for the meeting were met. Review the agenda to be sure you covered everything. Check your original CPS process starting point (depending on where in the process you started, this could be your statement of the goal, wish, challenge, your problem statement, or your solution statement) to make sure the session didn't go off on an unproductive tangent.

Follow-up plan
The unsung hero of many facilitated sessions is a follow-up plan. This simple "to do list" serves as a bridge to link the good ideas that came from the session to the good intentions written in the Plan of Action. The follow-up plan focuses on immediate post-meeting logistics. Use the same format as the Plan of Action (what will be done, by whom, by when, and reporting completion to whom), and put together a follow-up plan that addresses any actions steps resulting from the meeting. (See example on next page.)

This process may look slow to you, but I can promise you that no one ever asks that snappy little hare back to facilitate a session.

EXAMPLE of follow-up plan items:

Type up the notes

Distribute the results to people who need to know them

Research key issues

Share the Plan of Action with key individuals

Obtain approvals to proceed to next steps

Reserve conference room for next meeting

Schedule a follow-up meeting

Follow-up on the plan in a certain period of time
   (exactly how many days/weeks/months?)

Invite key participants to next meeting

Pay the facilitator

If these items aren't nailed down, everyone walks away assuming someone else will do them, and nothing happens. The result? Failure, despite a great facilitated session.

Evaluate

Finally, teams that work well together have one thing in common: They debrief what happened. They find out what worked well (so they can continue doing it) and what didn't work so well (so they can improve it). Debriefing benefits the group, the client and you—the facilitator. Reserve at least 5-15 minutes at the end of your session to evaluate what happened. Use Praise First to evaluate the pluses, potentials, concerns, and then, if necessary, spend a few minutes overcoming the concerns. You can either do this in a large group, scribing on a flip chart, or have participants fill out individual evaluation sheets. Take the time (and the risk) to debrief every meeting. It's a sure-fire strategy for improving your facilitation skills and the group's performance.

Debriefing (in brief)

- What worked well?
- What would you do differently?
- What did you learn or relearn?
- What learnings would you apply next time?

FACILITATION

Stages of Group Development

As a facilitator, you will be expected to handle CPS process, but you will also be expected to handle group process—better known as group dynamics. If nothing else, be aware that there are some basic stages every group passes through on its way to high performance. Bruce Tuckman examined and summarized the results of over 50 group development studies and created this four-stage model.

"Group process evolves naturally. It is self-regulating. Do not interfere. It will work itself out. Efforts to control process usually fail. Either they block process or make it chaotic. Learn to trust what is happening. If there is silence; let it grow; something will emerge. If there is a storm, let it rage; it will resolve into calm. Is the group discontented? You can't make it happy. Even if you could, your efforts might well deprive the group of a very creative struggle."

JOHN HEIDER
THE TAO OF LEADERSHIP

Forming
In the forming stage, the group is discovering and learning about each member. Group members test out behaviors and attitudes acceptable to other group members. There is a degree of ambiguity among group members and the task. Little progress is made on the task(s).

Storming
Storming is characterized by conflict among group members, who are more familiar with each other and the task at hand. This results in tension and competition among group members. Little progress is made on the task.

Norming
In the norming stage, the group begins to accept norms, roles and one another. The task at hand becomes clearer. Conflicts are dealt with effectively and a sense of cohesiveness is reached. Progress is made on the task.

Performing
Performing is characterized by progress and team work. Group members are focused on achieving success in completing the task while maintaining positive interpersonal relationships. A great deal of progress is made on completing the task.

Tuckman, B.W. (1965). Developmental sequence in small groups. *Psychological Bulletin, 63,* 384-399.

FACILITATION

Team Effectiveness
Stages of group development

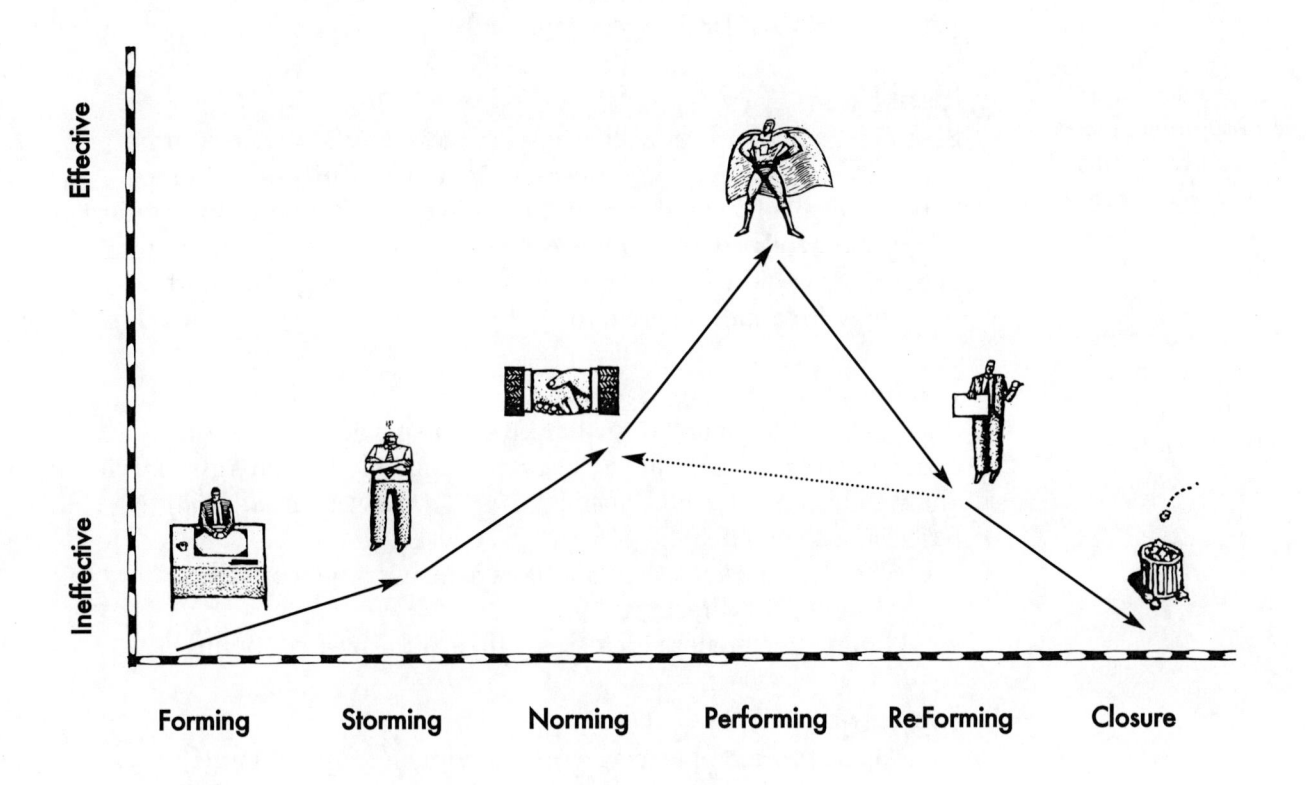

Y-axis: Ineffective → Effective
X-axis: Forming, Storming, Norming, Performing, Re-Forming, Closure

The chart above demonstrates the relationship between group development and group effectiveness. Note that this chart includes two additional stages of group development:

Reforming
Reforming occurs when a new piece of data is interjected at the performing stage. This data may be anything from a new group member to a change in task. In this stage, regrouping occurs. Group effectiveness tends to drop.

Closure
Closure occurs when the group has achieved its goal or is dissolved. In closure, the group debriefs and celebrates its experiences.

© 2011 Miller, Vehar, Firestien, Thurber, Nielsen

FACILITATION

Group Size
Too Big, Too Small, Just Right

Group size affects the dynamics and outcome of a meeting. As you work with groups, pay close attention to the group size that works best for your facilitation style.

Ideal Size
Based on experience, as well as research by experts such as Marvin Shaw, Scott Isaksen, Roger Firestien, Donald Treffinger and Sidney Parnes, the ideal facilitator-to-group ratio is one facilitator for a group of approximately five to nine people. If you have more than nine people in a session, consider breaking into two sub-groups and working with another facilitator.

Too Small
If the group is too small (less than five), the participants work extremely hard to generate ideas and can quickly lose energy. Marvin Shaw, in his book *Group Dynamics: The Psychology of Small Group Behavior*, also notes that:
- When groups are too small, there is heavy reliance on the facilitator for direction.
- Group effectiveness increases with group size (to a point).

Too Large
Shaw also reported obstacles working with a group too large:
- As group size increases, group members participate less.
- Group members feel more inhibited and threatened as group size increases.
- Group members feel less affinity for a larger group, and less satisfied with results.
- Smaller groups are more cohesive. Larger groups lead to greater disagreement among members.
- Larger groups have greater difficulty achieving consensus, hence there is more pressure towards group unity and conformity to group standards.

> "Smile... Many problems with group dynamics can be overcome easily with a combination of good basic training in the guidelines and a good sense of humor to reinforce positive group behavior."
>
> SUSAN KELLER-MATHERS

Using the CPS Process

If the wrong person uses the right means, the right means work in the wrong way.

ANCIENT CHINESE SAYING

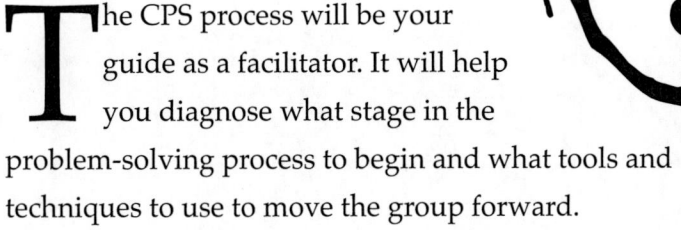

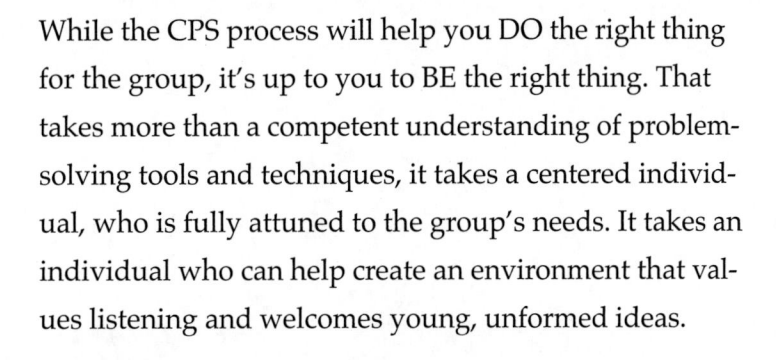

The CPS process will be your guide as a facilitator. It will help you diagnose what stage in the problem-solving process to begin and what tools and techniques to use to move the group forward.

While the CPS process will help you DO the right thing for the group, it's up to you to BE the right thing. That takes more than a competent understanding of problem-solving tools and techniques, it takes a centered individual, who is fully attuned to the group's needs. It takes an individual who can help create an environment that values listening and welcomes young, unformed ideas.

Ironically, the more you practice using CPS, the more "doing" the right thing becomes instinctual, and you can concentrate on "being" the right facilitator for the group. That's the stage of mastery where facilitators consistently exceed the expectations of their clients.

FACILITATION

Notes:

Know the process, but don't be its prisoner.

FACILITATION

The FourSight® Model
Moving from Basic to Expert

The basic model

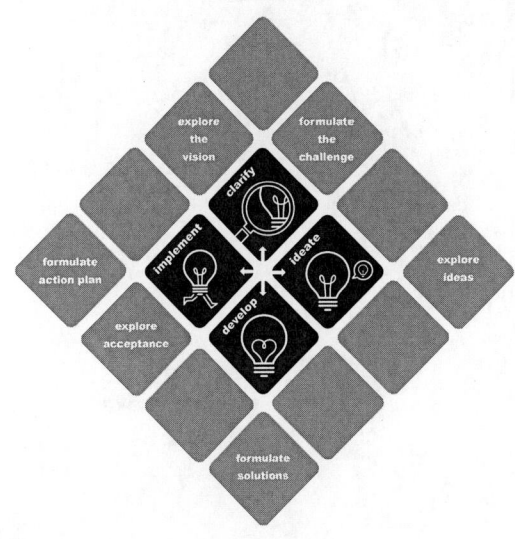

The expert model

When you're ready to lead others through the CPS process, you need to move from the basic FourSight model to the expert model.

The expert model presented here is based on a combination of FourSight and the Thinking Skills Model developed by Gerard Puccio, director of the International Center for Studies in Creativity in Buffalo, NY.

This expert model has three great advantages over the basic FourSight model: 1) it breaks the four steps of the FourSight model into more specific substeps for the facilitator, 2) it puts arrows at the center of the model to remind you to "assess the situation" on an ongoing basis, and 3) it associates each step with a thinking skill and an "affective" or feeling skill, to help the facilitator and the group know what frame of mind to strive for during the step.

To sum up the advantages:

1) adds substeps
2) puts "assess" in the center
3) connects to thinking and affective skills

© 2011 Miller, Vehar, Firestien, Thurber, Nielsen

FACILITATION

The Expert Model

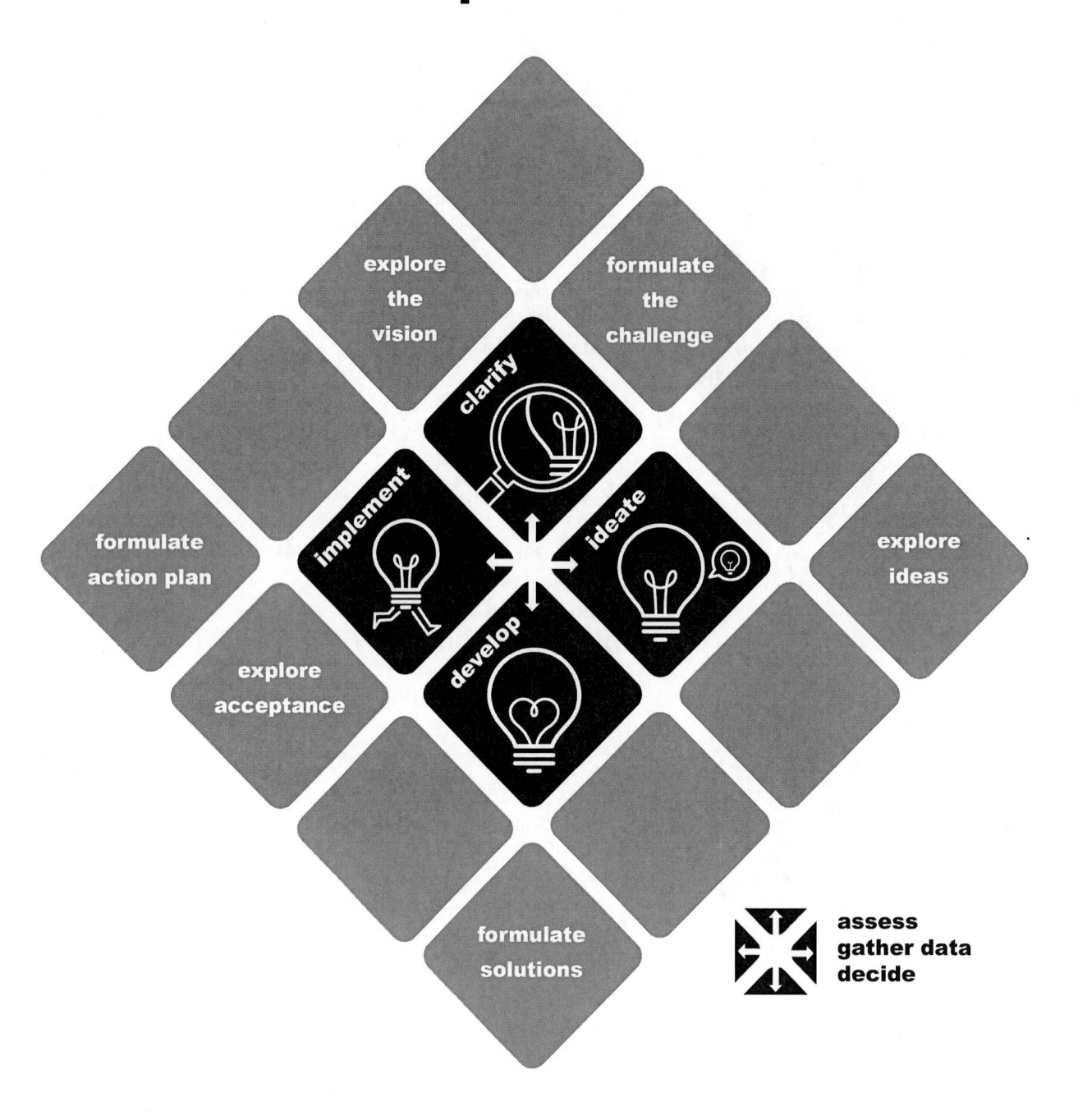

- explore the vision
- formulate the challenge
- formulate action plan
- explore ideas
- explore acceptance
- formulate solutions

- clarify
- ideate
- develop
- implement

assess
gather data
decide

FACILITATION

The Executive Step

In the center of the model

When you facilitate, you've got to think about your own thinking...

The expert model puts Assess the Sitation in the center of things and calls it "the executive step." That's because this step allows you to stand above the other steps and determine where to go in the process. It calls for "metacognition," meaning that you, the facilitator, have to think about your thinking.

Assess the Situation is the gateway into all the other steps.

FACILITATION

Assess the Situation
Gather data, then decide

Begin here.
When you assess the situation, you gather data to make decisions about how to proceed.

What counts as data?
Sources of data include facts, figures, intuitions, feelings and stories. Use that data to decide where to begin. Since there's no set way to move through the model, you can decide whether to explore the vision or explore ideas, formulate challenges or formulate solutions, etc. With practice, you'll know just where to go and how to lead your client on a worthwhile path through the process.

Your job:
Identify the relevant data to determine the next process step

Diverge:
Gather information from both objective sources (observations, facts, senses) and subjective sources (hunches, feelings, opinions, stories).

Converge:
Work with the client to choose the most relevant data. Create logical clusters of data to include on a poster for the session.

Output:
- A decision about where to begin in the CPS process
- A flip chart poster with key data points to share during the session.

With the client
Look at the goal, wish or challenge your client selected. What's known about it? What are all the facts, feelings and questions that surround it? Who's involved? Why is it an opportunity? Explore information relevant to this goal, wish or challenge. Remind the client that data is more than information and facts—it's also feelings, observations, questions and hunches. Ask open-ended questions like those on the following page.

FACILITATION

DATA QUESTIONS to ask the client:

- What is a brief history of the situation?
- Who is involved?
- Who is the decision maker?
- How do you own this situation?
- Who might gain if the situation is resolved?
- What successes have been achieved so far?
- What has promoted those successes?
- What are some of the obstacles you encountered?
- Where have you found help?
- When does this situation seem to occur?
- When would you like to see action taken on this situation?
- How long has it been a concern?
- Why is this a concern for you?
- How might this be an opportunity for you?
- What have you already thought of or tried?
- What other data is relevant to this situation?
- What are your gut feelings about it?
- How are your feelings affecting your behavior?
- What is your ideal outcome?

Facilitator Notes
- *Remind the client that even the "obvious" data is relevant.*
- *Transfer the key data onto blank sheets of flip chart paper.*

Finish with a "KEY DATA" poster: Write the key data in bullet point form on a flip chart.

Key Data
- data
- data
- data
- data
- data
- data
- data
- data
- data
- data
- data
- data

© 2011 Miller, Vehar, Firestien, Thurber, Nielsen

FACILITATION

Explore the Vision
Identify the goal, wish or challenge

TOOLS
- Brainstorming
- Excursion

STARTERS
It would be great if... IWBGI
I wish.... IW

Enter this step when...
...you want to help your client create a vision of what's possible. "Explore the Vision" is truly an exploratory stage. By diverging and converging on possible goals, wishes or challenges, your client may end up tackling a different challenge than the one they originally brought to the table.

Your job:
Help the client create a clear vision of a desired outcome

Diverge:
Encourage the client to list of goals, wishes and challenges. Use the questions on the next page to help them articulate a range of options. Come up with a whole series of phrases starting with "It would be great if..." or "I wish...."

Converge:
Help your client chose one goal/wish/challenge statement.

With the client
Before you converge, check that the client truly has ownership, motivation and a need for imagination by asking them to look over the list of goal/wish/challenge statements and put a check by each statement, each time it meets one of the following criteria*:

Ownership
You have influence and accountability for the situation.

Motivation
You really want to take action on it.

Imagination
It requires novelty or new thinking.

Statements with three check marks are good candidates for CPS.

Output:
- A single goal/wish/challenge statement that begins with "I wish... or "It would be great if..."
- A flip chart poster to share during the session

FACILITATION

VISION QUESTIONS to ask the client:

- What things have you done lately that you'd like to do better?
- What sorts of challenges might be on your mind?
- What do you wish worked better?
- Who has been on your mind lately? Why?
- What are some objectives that you would like to meet?
- Scan your life. What opportunities would you like to take advantage of?
- Imagine yourself one year from today. What goals, dreams or visions would you like to accomplish or begin in the next year?
- You've just been given a magic wand. Any wish in your life can come true. What might some of those ideal goals or wishes be?

Facilitator Notes
- *Write down the client's goal, wish or challenge in their own words. (Have them say it as a headline if necessary.)*
- *If the client can't settle on one item to work on, ask which one is most immediate.*

It would be great if IWBGI... or I wish IW...

Finish with a "VISION" poster: Write your client's goal, wish or challenge statement on a flip chart

© 2011 Miller, Vehar, Firestien, Thurber, Nielsen

FACILITATION

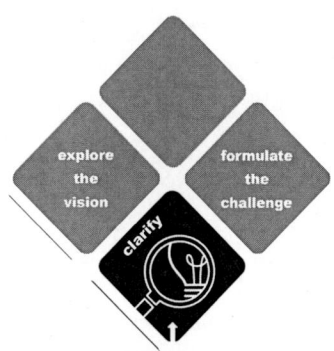

Formulate the Challenge

Decide on what problem to solve

TOOLS
- Phrase problems as questions
- Why? What's stopping you?

STARTERS
How to... H2
How might... HM
In what ways might... IWWM
What might be all the... WMBAT

Enter this step when...
...you've gathered data, assessed the situation and have a broad vision that begins with the phrase "I wish..." or "It would be great if..." Now it's time to get specific: Given the vision, exactly what challenge are you going to address?

Your job:
Help the client pinpoint the right challenge to address

Diverge:
Have the client and/or resource group restate the issue from as many perspectives as possible. Use the statement starters: *"How to...?" "How might...?" "In what ways might...?"* or *"What might be all the...?"* If you get stuck, look again at the key data and try to make problem statements based on the data. Go for at least 25 to 30 different statements.

Converge:
Choose a single challenge to work on. If the client sees one challenge standing head and shoulders above the rest, the group can move on to Generate Ideas. If not, use a convergent tool like highlighting.

With the client
Check in with the client after some statements have been generated. Ask, "Are we getting something for you?" or "Are we heading in the right direction?"

Output:
- A single, well-defined statement of the challenge
- A flip chart poster with the challenge statement at the top

FACILITATION

INTEGRATING the group into the CPS process:

Often, "Formulate the Challenge" is the step where the client and resource group start working together. Some brief introductions may be appropriate. Take a moment with the group to review:

- The roles in a CPS session
- Ground rules for diverging and converging
- The use of statement starters

You might ask the client to help bring the group up to speed by explaining the flip chart that lists the statement of the goal, wish or challenge and the key data. Ask the group if they have any questions for the client that will help them better understand the situation.

Facilitator Notes
- *If the flow of problem statements slows down, try a divergent thinking tool, such as "Why? What's Stopping You?" or Word Dance.*
- *Praise and encourage the resource group when they are diverging. Tell them, "You all are doing a great job!" or "Keep the energy level up!"*

How to...?
　How might...
In what ways
　might... or
What might be
　all the...

Finish with a "CHALLENGE" poster:
Write your client's challenge
statement on top of a flip chart

FACILITATION

Explore Ideas
Generate lots (and lots) of options

TOOLS:
Brainstorming
Brainwriting
SCAMPER
Forced Connections
Visual Connections
Excursions

STARTERS
What I see myself
[us] doing is...

Enter this step when...
...you have a clearly defined challenge, and you need ideas to solve it. Remember, the best way to come up with great ideas is to generate LOTS of ideas. The mind only starts getting creative once the obvious answers are covered. So, be generous with your own and other people's ideas: Defer judgment. Build off other ideas. Freewheel and stretch for outlandish ideas. It's easier to tame a wild idea than to energize a dull one. Go beyond the obvious. Strive for quantity.

Your job:
Help the group generate *lots* of options, ideas and possibilities

Diverge:
Think up a wide variety of ideas to address the challenge. But first, ask the client to read aloud the vision statement, the key data and the challenge statement to the group. Reinforce the guidelines for divergent thinking.

Have the resource group come up with at least 35 ideas that might solve the client's problem. Go for 35 more. Even as you see good ideas emerge, keep pushing the group for novelty. Stretch! (Use questions on next page.) Keep going until the client says they have enough ideas.

Converge:
Choose the most promising ideas. Combine them into a narrative description that begins, "What I see myself [us] doing is..."

With the client
Check in with the client after some statements have been generated. Ask, "Are we getting something for you?" or "Are we heading in the right direction?"

Output:
Selected ideas that address the challenge, plus a written paragraph that begins, "What I see myself [us] doing is..." This narrative should detail specific actions, people, dates and measurable results, so that a stranger could clearly understand the intended solution.

FACILITATION

QUESTIONS to ask the group:

Use SCAMPER questions to jog the imagination:

Substitute: What process, people or materials can you substitute?
Combine: How can you combine parts, people or processes?
Adapt: What else is like this?
Modify: What can you add, subtract, modify or change?
Put to other uses: What other uses might there be for this?
Eliminate: What can you get rid of, sacrifice or omit?
Rearrange: What other patterns or arrangements can you try?

Use a Forced Connections phrase:
"When you look at this (object or picture), what ideas do you get for solving this problem?"

Facilitator Notes

- *Remember to number the flip chart pages.*
- *To clarify an idea ask, "What's your thinking on that?"*
- *Consider taking a short stretch break. Keep the energy level up.*
- *If the flow of ideas slows down, use a divergent tool, such as brainwriting, forced connections, visual connections or SCAMPER.*
- *Check in with the resource group while the client converges. Remind them that they are important.*

Finish with a "SOLUTION" poster:
Write your client's solution statement on top of a flip chart.

> What I see myself [us] doing is...

© 2011 Miller, Vehar, Firestien, Thurber, Nielsen

FACILITATION

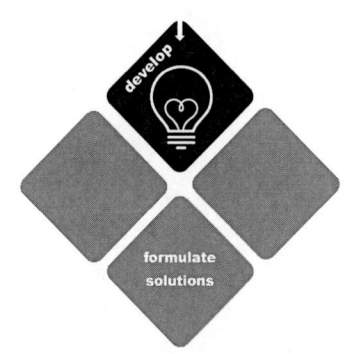

Formulate Solutions
Select and strengthen solutions

TOOLS:
POINt
Card Sort
Evaluation Matrix
Targeting
Prototyping

STARTERS
What I NOW see myself [us] doing is...

Enter this step when...
...you have a solution statement that incorporates you most promising ideas, and the client is ready to analyze and improve them.

Your job:
Help the group refine and develop a more robust solution

Diverge:
If there is one solution, generate a list of pluses, opportunities, issues and ways to overcome any issues. If there are diverse solutions, generate critiera to evaluate them.

Converge:
Select the best new thinking that helps overcome any issues. Prioritize your diverse solutions. Make incremental improvements.

With the client
If the client has developed criteria for the solution's success, be sure to hold the emerging solution against those criteria.

Output:
An addendum to your solution statement, starting with the phrase "What I NOW see myself [us] doing is..."

© 2011 Miller, Vehar, Firestien, Thurber, Nielsen

FACILITATION

QUESTIONS to ask the client:
Use Praise First (POINt) to strengthen ideas.

Pluses: What are the things you like about it—the advantages?

Opportunities: What would become possible in the future if this came to pass? What are the spin-offs or possible future gains? (Use the statement starter: "It might...")

Issues: What are possible limitations?
(Be sure to pose these as questions: "How to...," "How might...,"
"In what ways might..." or "What might be all the...")

New Thinking: Overcome issues one at a time, in order of their importance to the client.

Facilitator Notes
- *Encourage the resource group to keep the end user in mind. Is the solution you're developing meeting their needs?*

Finish with a "DEVELOPED SOLUTION" poster: Write your client's additional solution statement on top of a flip chary.

What I NOW see myself [us] doing is...

FACILITATION

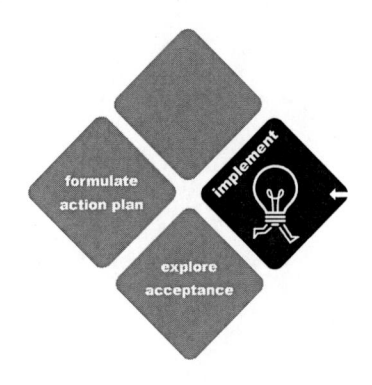

Explore Acceptance
Putting the solution in context

TOOLS:
- Assisters & Resisters
- Stakeholder Analysis

Enter this step when...
...you have a fully developed solution. It looks good on flip charts, but you want buy-in from people and the intended environment.

Your job:
Help the client analyze what forces will help and hinder the implementation of the solution

Diverge:
Make a list of "assisters," who could help make your solution work. Include specific ways in which you could enlist their help. Make a list of "resisters," and include ways to overcome their resistance.

Converge:
Select which assisters and resisters you will focus on.

With the client
This is a step many people gloss over, to the detriment of their solution. Encourage your client and the resource group to take a bit of time here to do the job well. It will save heartache (and often dollars) in the long run.

Output:
- A list of assisters and resisters to incorporate into the action plan
- A list of specific strategies for gaining or maintaining their support

FACILITATION

QUESTIONS to ask the group:

- Who might assist you with your solution?
- Who needs to be convinced about the merits of your solution?
- What steps might you take to put your solution into action?
- What resources are available (people, materials, money)?
- How can we gain acceptance for this solution?
- How can we build enthusiasm?
- What are some things you might need to work to overcome?
- Where might you start?
- What special places or locations might you use?
- What are locations to avoid?
- How might you pre-test this solution?
- What are some contingencies you might develop for your idea?

Facilitator Notes
- *Once again, encourage the resource group to keep the end in mind — not only the end user, but the environment in which the solution will live.*

Finish with a "ACCEPTANCE" poster: The simplest is this 2-column format.

Assisters	Resisters

© 2011 Miller, Vehar, Firestien, Thurber, Nielsen

FACILITATION

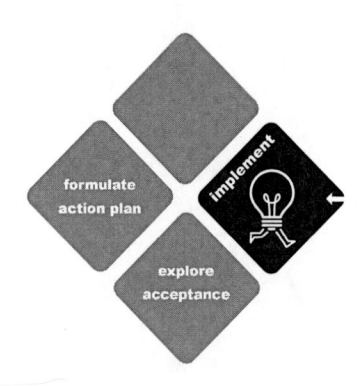

Formulate Action Plan

The ultimate "to do" list

TOOLS:
- Action Planning
- Debriefing Questions

Enter this step when...
...you are ready to implement the solution

Your job:
Help the client focus on actions that will make this solution a reality.

Diverge:
Generate a list of everything that needs to be done. Include steps that involve acceptance and resistance.

Converge:
Draw up a list of who will do what by when, reporting completion to whom.

With the client
Review the diverged list of action items. Remove those that are not essential to the solution. Combine steps that fit together. Sequence the steps in terms of short-term, mid-term and long-term planning. Finally, decide on one item that the client will commit to doing in the next 24-hours. Implementation is all about momentum!

Output:
- A plan that details who does what by when, reporting to whom
- A commitment to a task to complete within 24 hours

FACILITATION

QUESTIONS to ask the group:

- What short-term actions do you need to take?
- What mid-term actions do you need to take?
- What long-term actions do you need to take?
- What can you do in the next 24 hours?
- How can you maintain enthusiasm for this solution?

DEBRIEFING QUESTIONS for the group to ask themselves as they implement the solution:

- What worked?
- What could we have improved or done better?
- What should we do next time?

Facilitator Notes
- Create a chart like the one at right. List each action step individually and detail who will do it, when it must be completed, and who needs to know that it's done.
- In addition to the action plan, be sure to draw up a "follow-up plan" for the session. See page 38-39 for suggestions.

Finish with an "ACTION PLAN" poster

ACTION PLAN			
Action	by whom?	by when?	reporting to whom?
short-term			
mid-term			
long-term			
In 24 hours...			

FACILITATION

Thinking Skills

Some cognitive skills associated with each step*

Assess the Situation takes Diagnostic Thinking	Making a careful examination of the situation, describing the nature of the problem, deciding what process steps to take
Explore the Vision takes Visionary Thinking	Articulating a vivid image of your desired outcome
Formulate the Challenge takes Strategic Thinking	Identifying the critical issues to address and paths forward to a desired future state
Explore Ideas takes Ideational Thinking	Producing original mental images and thoughts in response to challenges
Formulate Solutions takes Evaluative Thinking	Assessing the reasonableness and quality of ideas in order to develop workable solutions
Explore Acceptance takes Contextual Thinking	Understanding the linking conditions and circumstances that will support or hinder an success
Formulate Action Plan takes Tactical Thinking	Devising a plan that includes specific, measurable steps to reach a goal, plus methods to measure effectiveness

* *Drawn from "Creative Leadership: Skills that drive change" (2nd ed.) by Gerard Puccio, Marie Mance and Marie Murdock at Buffalo State, State University of New York.*

FACILITATION

Affective Skills

Some affective (or "feeling") skills associated with each step*

Assess the Situation takes Mindfulness	Attending to thoughts, feelings and sensations relative to the present situation
Explore the Vision takes Dreaming	To imaging as possible your desires, hopes and dreams
Formulate the Challenge takes Sensing Gaps	To be continuously aware of the difference between what is and what could be
Explore Ideas takes Playfulness	Freely toying with ideas and possibilities
Formulate Solutions takes Avoiding Premature Closure	Resisting the urge to push for a final decision
Explore Acceptance takes Sensitivity to Environment	The degree to which people are aware of their physical and psychological surroundings
Formulate Action Plan takes Tolerance for Risk	Not allowing yourself to be shaken or unnerved by the possibility of failure or setbacks

* *Drawn from "Creative Leadership: Skills that drive change" (2nd ed.) by Gerard Puccio, Marie Mance and Marie Murdock at Buffalo State, State University of New York.*

© 2011 Miller, Vehar, Firestien, Thurber, Nielsen

FACILITATION

CPS Toolbox to... Diverge

Tool	Use when ...	CPS stage
Brainstorming	You want to generate many options with a group.	• Any stage
Brainwriting	You want to generate options or incremental improvements. Great for groups that have trouble deferring judgment or speaking out.	• Any stage
Forced Connections	You need to stretch thinking in an idea generating session.	• Explore Ideas • Formulate Challenge
"Why? What's Stopping You?"	You want to generate statements of the problem with either a broader or narrower perspective.	• Formulate Challenge • Explore Ideas
Open-Ended Questions	You want to stimulate thinking and generate options or get more group interaction.	• Explore the Vision • Gather Data
Plan for Action Questions	You want to generate specific action steps.	• Formulate Action Plan
SCAMPER	You need to stretch thinking and generate many options.	• Explore Ideas
Visual Connections	You want to stretch thinking in a brainstorming session, especially to produce innovative options.	• Explore Ideas • Formulate Challenge • Formulate Solutions

© 2011 Miller, Vehar, Firestien, Thurber, Nielsen

FACILITATION

CPS Toolbox to... Converge

Tool	Use when ...	CPS stage
Card Sort	You have many options to narrow down and want to prioritize them.	• Formulate Challenge • Explore Ideas • Formulate Solutions
Highlighting (hits, cluster, restate)	You have many options that need to be narrowed down and grouped by theme.	• Formulate Challenge • Explore Ideas • Formulate Action Plan
Hits	You have a few options that stand "head-and-shoulders" above the rest.	• Any stage
Evaluation Matrix	You have many options to select and evaluate using criteria.	• Formulate Solutions
Praise First POINt (pluses, opportunities, issues, new thinking)	You have one or a few options to consider.	• Formulate Solutions
Targeting	You have one or more strong options and want to strengthen or evaluate them.	• Explore the Vision • Formulate Challenge • Explore Ideas • Formulate Solutions

© 2011 Miller, Vehar, Firestien, Thurber, Nielsen

FACILITATION

Facilitator Cheat Sheet

Stage	Explore the Vision	Gather Data	Formulate the Challenge
Purpose	Identify situations & challenges that require improvement	Explore key data from many viewpoints	Explore the problem to focus problem-solving efforts
Diagnosis	Is the situation unclear? Is the direction clear?	Do you know everything about the situation? Do you need additional information?	Is the problem well defined? Are there other approaches that might solve the problem better?
Inputs	Need to establish a goal or focus for problem solving	An area that needs to be explored for further data (typically a goal/wish/challenge statement)	An issue that needs to be focused (typically a goal/wish/challenge statement)
To do	Generate goal/wish challenge statements; converge on one statement to explore	Generate who, what, when, where, why (5Ws) and how data; converge on key data	Generate specific problem statements & converge on one problem statement
Statement starters	I wish... It would be great if...(IWBGI)	None	In what ways might...(IWWM) How to... (H2) How might... (HM) What might be all the...(WMBAT)
Diverge	Open-ended questions Brainstorming	5 W's Open-ended questions Brainstorming	Brainstorming "Why? What's Stopping You?" Word Dance
Converge	Hits Highlighting	Hits	Hits Highlighting
Outcome	A goal/wish/challenge statement that requires further exploration	A list of key data that will help to generate problem statements	A well-defined problem statement to be used for generating ideas

F-66

© 2011 Miller, Vehar, Firestien, Thurber, Nielsen

FACILITATION

Explore Ideas	Formulate Solutions	Explore Acceptance	Formulate Action Plan
Create novel and useful ideas that address the challenge	Strengthen ideas for meeting the challenge	Anticipate factors that will assist and resist your solution	Develop a plan of action to implement
Do you know how to solve your problem? Do you need novel & unique solutions?	Do you have a fully developed solution? Do you know the best solution?	Have you accounted for all the key people, time, locations, etc.?	How will you implement the solution?
A problem that requires novel & unique solutions	A solution(s) that needs to be evaluated & strengthened	A clear statement of "What you see yourself doing"	A fully developed solution that needs a plan to make it happen.
Generate many varied ideas and converge on those that solve the challenge	Evaluate and strengthen ideas with Praise First or Evaluation Matrix	Think through who and what lies ahead Generate a list and converge on key factors	Ask the 5W's. Use the answers to brainstorm action steps. Chart who will do what by when, reporting to whom
None	What I see myself (us) doing is... Will it ... Does it... Is it... What I *now* see myself (us) doing is...	None	None
Brainstorming Visual Connections Brainwriting, SCAMPER Forced Connections	Brainstorming	Assisters/Resisters Stakeholder Analysis	Brainstorming Open-ended questions Plan for Action questions
Highlighting Hits	Praise First (POINt) Evaluation Matrix Card Sort, Targeting	Hits	Hits
One idea or a selected list of ideas that will resolve the problem	Fully thought-out and analyzed solutions	A key list of assisters and resisters to put into your action plan	A plan of action for implementing solutions

© 2011 Miller, Vehar, Firestien, Thurber, Nielsen

FACILITATION

Notes:

Unusual props and toys help infuse energy and imagination in a group setting. We suggest choosing these items carefully.

Advanced Facilitation Tips

> "If all you have is a hammer,
> then everything looks like a nail."
>
> — ABRAHAM MASLOW

Knowing the stages of the problem-solving process is only the first step. The facilitator must not only know which phase is appropriate, but which tool is best suited to get the job done and what technique will most benefit the group.

The following pages contain tips for being a "hero facilitator" as well as charts that cross-reference tools and process stages. These advanced skills and cheatsheets may help out in a pinch.

FACILITATION

Facilitator All-Star Tips (FAST)

Be the best darn facilitator you can be

There you are, standing proudly in front of a group of eager participants. They look at you admiringly...the facilitator. When suddenly, the flip chart crashes to the floor. You're out of flip chart paper! The markers are dried up! You've lost the masking tape!

We've seen it—sessions losing momentum and energy due to inattention to details. What follows is a compilation of lessons learned (the hard way). This essential "to do" list will ensure that your facilitation will go as smoothly as possible without getting sidetracked by logistics. We pass these tips along in hopes of sparing you the embarrassment of learning them yourself. And by the way, you're welcome!

Your resource group will love you for this.

Setting up

Hang the presentation charts in advance
Prepare the agenda, roles, guidelines, data and task summary ahead of time. Hang them in advance in an easily seen place, preferably on the wall towards the front of the room, high enough so that another flip chart can easily fit underneath. Pick a place that will catch people's attention.

Secure the flip chart
Double check to make sure the flip chart stand is stable and that the flip chart pad is firmly in place. Tear off a dozen 2" or 3" strips of masking tape and stick them on the back of the flip chart so the tape is ready to go when it's time to hang the flip chart pages.

Number the flip charts
A high-energy CPS session can result in dozens, even hundreds, of idea-laden flip chart pages. Avoid flip chart chaos. Number each flip chart page consecutively and put a heading in the corner. For example, if you start a session in the Gather Data stage and then

move on to the Explore the Vision stage, your flip charts might be numbered something like this:

> Gather Data 1
> Gather Data 2
> Explore Vision 3
> Explore Vision 4

Use whatever notation makes sense to you and your client so the pages are easily readable and can be sorted after the session.

Decide where to hang the flip chart pages
If your session generates reams of flip chart paper, what will you do with it? Know the answer before you start the session. Scout out the room and anticipate scenarios. Plan on hanging flip chart pages about eye level so that people can get up, walk around and reflect on the ideas if necessary. (Don't forget to hang your presentation flip chart pages—agenda, roles and ground rules—in front of the room before the session starts.)

Have timers available
A timer is an easy, effective way to bring groups back to focus and keep track of how much time is dedicated to each activity. We like the big digital timers with large, easy-to-read numbers.

Double check supplies
Do I have enough post-it pads, pens and markers? Do my markers work? Do I have "Forced Connections" objects or pictures? Double check before the session. A few well spent minutes in preparation can make the difference between a fumbled facilitation and a fabulous one.

FACILITATION

Facilitator as Hero

Brilliant moves during the session

Like any life skill, the better you get at the basics, the more attention you can pay to the details. And details are often what distinguish the yeoman from the hero facilitator. As you gain more experience facilitating, pay attention to the following:

> "It has long been an axiom of mine that the little things are infinitely the most important."
>
> ARTHUR CONAN DOYLE

Know when to facilitate and when to teach.
Before you use a CPS tool, teach the group what the tool is and how it works. A good facilitator, therefore, is also a good teacher. Make sure you teach participants the tools and techniques they will be using in a CPS session. Show them examples and give them time to practice these techniques on challenges that are unrelated to the actual problem. Let participants see the tools in action before they are required to try them on a difficult situation. We recommend that even if you only have a short time to facilitate a session, say 4 hours, that you spend the first 45 to 60 minutes training the group in the techniques they will use later in the session. Ideally, participants will have attended a basic course in Creative Problem Solving before they take on a tough challenge. But even if they have, take some time reviewing the CPS process and give the group a brief warm-up exercise before tackling the challenge. It's time well spent.

Monitor your nonverbal messages.
Have you ever listened to someone whose body language contradicted their words? Did you find their message believable? Body language can either reinforce or undermine the credibility of verbal language. According to the communication researcher, Dr. Albert Mehrabian, over 90 percent of both our positive and negative meaning is conveyed by tone of voice, body expressions and gestures. When you facilitate a session, don't just say what you mean, reinforce it with nonverbal gestures and vocal inflections. Your entire body can convey the message you want to send—but if you're not careful, it might be conveying messages you don't want to send. Pay attention to nonverbal communication, your own and your group's.

Watch your energy level.
Groups will pick up and reflect your energy level. If the group seems a little low on enthusiasm, be full of energy yourself. The group will rise to your level. You'll have more fun. The group will have more fun, and pretty soon they'll be sending energy your way.

FACILITATION

What do you mean they want to carve a facilitator next to Lincoln!?

What's a facilitator?

Don't hover.
Groups react to whether you are standing or sitting. When a small group is getting disruptive or off track, walk over and "visit" them. Just walking near a group is often enough to get them back on task. When participants are working in small groups or on individual tasks, it's not necessary to walk around and "check" on them. Adult learners don't appreciate being watched over. If groups appear to be on task, sit down and let them work. They will appreciate the space.

Set a quota.
Research has shown—and experience has proven—that simply setting a quota for how many ideas or problem statements you want a group to generate will push them to stretch further than they ordinarily would. And the more ideas you generate, the greater your chances of coming up with good ideas. Remember, an effective brainstorming session is not generating four ideas in five minutes. It's generating 40 or 50 or 60 ideas in five minutes. Setting the bar at a high, but achievable quota gives a group a common goal to reach and leaves them feeling energized and productive.

Check in with the client.
Want to be sure the session is headed in the right direction? Just ask! Checking in with the client is a brief, powerful way to ensure a smooth session. Every so often, ask the client "Are we going in the

FACILITATION

right direction? Are we getting the type of ideas you want? Do you feel we have enough ideas?" Depending on the client's answers, you may follow up with "Is there another direction you'd like to go?" This gives the client a chance to express feedback during the session, making everyone's time more productive and satisfying.

Don't abandon a converging client.
When the diverging is done, it's tempting to give the resource group a break and let the client deliberate over the options alone. Don't do it. Keep the resource group in the room while the client is converging so they are available to answer any questions the client may have about their ideas. Keeping the group nearby also sends the nonverbal message that they are supportive of the client.

Use leveling to manage group conversation.
During a facilitation, there may be times you want to ignite group discussion. If you want to encourage people to talk more, come down to their level—physically. After you ask them a question, sit down so you are eye level with the group. Chances are, the group will begin to open up. When you are standing, the group tends to perceive you as an authoritarian figure. When you sit, you appear more of an equal, and people will tend to speak more freely.

Take time out when you need it.
Sometimes things don't go as planned. If this happens during a session, don't be afraid to take some time to readjust the session plan. Give the group a short break, or ask the group to spend a few minutes discussing their key insights in the session so far. Use the time to check in with your client, revisit your plan and make any necessary changes. A few well spent minutes can make a big difference.

"I brake for inappropriate behavior."
It's rare to have to stop a session to deal with inappropriate behavior, but occasionally it happens. If you find that an individual is disrupting the session and inhibiting the learning of others, take a short break and talk to that person in private. Find out if something is troubling them. Then take steps to solve the problem. It's often not the session at all, but a pressing business or personal issue.

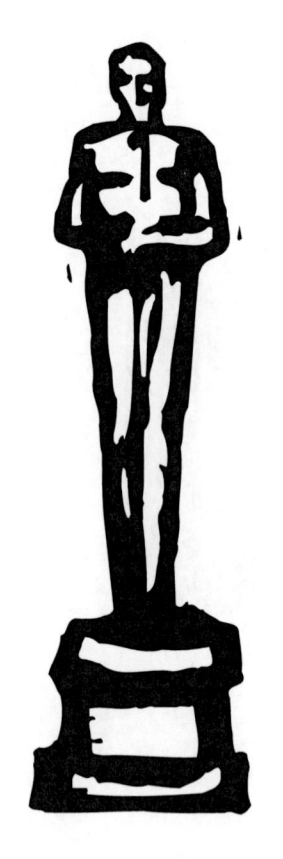

I'd like to thank my CPS trainers, my clients and my resource group.

FACILITATION

Don't short change solution statements.
While the desire for clarity and brevity remains, remember that CPS sessions are usually convened to address complex problems, and complex problems often have complex solutions. Be flexible. If a solution has many parts, make sure all the parts are captured eloquently. The solution statement should encapsulate the nuances of the solution. A solution statement can be as long or short as necessary, but it should be detailed enough to lead to action. For example, if a new widget needs to be marketed, a brief solution statement might read:

"What I see myself doing is marketing this widget to grocery stores."

This solution statement is too general to capture all the ideas discussed in the session. A better solution statement might read:

"What we see ourselves doing first is hiring BCX corporation to conduct a competitive analysis of the widget market. Second, we will take the results of that report, analyze them and formulate our initial marketing strategy. Third, we will have two-day retreat, bringing in key leaders from around the country to get insights from all 50 departments of the company. Fourth, we will spend six weeks visiting all the grocers in the Northeast part of the state, gathering their firsthand feedback. Fifth, we will compile all our data and insights into our final marketing strategy. Finally, we will introduce the widget over a four-month roll-out starting with grocery stores in the Northeast part of the state.

Not all solutions are simple.

FACILITATION

Facilitator Speak

Say the magic words

Every facilitator faces that moment of truth when the group runs out of ideas, the client runs out of patience and the facilitator just wants to yell, "Can't you dopes think of something?!?" But this is not the way of the wise facilitator. This is the moment the group needs your confidence and encouragement the most. Having a gentle phrase or probing question can help get the ideas flowing again. Consider the following:

Abracadabra, is it?

For checking in with the client:
Are we going in the right direction for you?
Are these on track?
Do you have enough ideas or would you like more?
Do you feel comfortable with this direction?
Do you have enough ideas to overcome that concern?
Are we on track here?
I want to check where we're at, at this point.
What's working?

Divergent Questions
What are all the ideas you can imagine for solving this?
Let's get more ideas for solving this.
What's stopping you?
Why?
Say more.
What is you thinking?
What is your image behind that?
Tell me more about that.
What is getting in the way?
Put yourself in the shoes of: (a child, the CEO, etc.)
So, if you had to summarize that, how would you say it?
Imagine yourself in that situation— what do you see?
What ideas do you get when you think about:…..?
What perspective would be the opposite of yours?
What are the assumptions we are making?
What is a contradictory response?
Imagine if…

FACILITATION

Let's stretch our thinking.
Picture yourself five years from today…
Let's stretch for two more minutes.
Keep 'em coming.
Let's dig a little deeper.
Great idea! Keep 'em coming.
So what are the common themes here?

Convergent Questions
Does that do it for you?
Any clarifying questions?
Do you want to continue discussing this or are you ready to move on?

Let's dig a little deeper…

Say more.

Put yourself in the shoes of a child…

FACILITATION

Selecting a Resource Group

Who's gonna do that CPS voodoo?

Your resource group will dramatically affect the outcome of the session. So pick wisely. Or more accurately, encourage your client to pick wisely. At first, many clients only want participants who really know the subject matter. That's a good place to start, but limiting the group to, say, members of the marketing department, will shrink the likelihood of getting fresh—and often useful—perspectives.

The ideal resource group has representatives from all departments or divisions in the organization, as well as customers, clients and people who know nothing whatsoever about the challenge.

The Great Resource Group

The Great Resource Group is made up of those who know the challenge area from every possible angle (yes, even accounting, manufacturing and shipping). The Group also includes those who haven't a clue about the subject matter and can ask "dumb" questions that provide brilliant insights to the problem. If possible, include creative outsiders who aren't afraid to bombard the group with wild ideas that may be completely off the mark. They can stimulate the group to think in new ways, to build off wild ideas and stretch. After all, you are looking for novel ideas, right?

You can search the world over looking for a perfect resource group.

FACILITATION

Consider inviting people from:

Marketing
Operations
Engineering
Finance
Line workers
Purchasing
Accounting
Transportation
Administrative
Manufacturing
Customer Service
Production
Software development
Product management
Management
Sales

Product development
Legal
Research & Development
Human Resources
Planning
Market Research
Customers
Consumers
End users
Suppliers
Peers in similar positions
Creative sparkplugs (e.g. freelance writers, artists, wild thinkers, teachers, children)

True tales: A snapshot

After taking photographs for a full day in 1943, Edwin Land's three-year-old daughter asked why she had to wait for the film to be processed. That "dumb" question inspired Polaroid's Land camera, which created nearly instant photos. Sometimes the simplest questions can provoke major breakthroughs.

FACILITATION

Notes:

It's a bird! It's a plane! It's a super FACILITATOR!

Appendix

The beginning...

FACILITATION

FACILITATION

CPS Facilitator Self Assessment

Mark what you believe is your current skill level on each dimension below. Use a scale from 1-10 (where 1 needs improvement, and 10 is outstanding). Then give yourself an overall rating on the section.

Teaching and Applying CPS Tools
____ Uses proper CPS terminology
____ Effectively presents CPS tools
____ Presents rationale for CPS tools
____ Encourages others to use tools appropriately
____ Provides comfortable transitions
____ Demonstrates confidence in CPS by sharing personal applications
____ Manages interactions of resource group and clients

1	2	3	4	5	6	7	8	9	10
Needs Improvement				Satisfactory			Outstanding		

Actions for development :

Conducting CPS Session and Session Preparation
____ Provides necessary resources (post-its, markers, tools, posters, forced connections, pictures, agenda, etc.)
____ Plans appropriate use of space (tables, seating, workspace, flip charts, display of charts, etc.)
____ Establishes agenda
____ Shares clear priorities and session objectives
____ Paces session appropriately
____ Manages information flow (records options etc.)
____ Uses tools effectively
____ Promotes development of an outcome that meets clients' needs
____ Establishes next steps from the session

1	2	3	4	5	6	7	8	9	10
Needs Improvement				Satisfactory			Outstanding		

Actions for development :

© 2011 Miller, Vehar, Firestien, Thurber, Nielsen

FACILITATION

Working with the Client
____ Conducts client interview (records meeting on worksheet)
____ Checks client's ownership of situation and related content
____ During session checks with client for appropriateness of direction
____ Encourages client openness and involvement in process
____ Supports client decisions during the CPS session

1	2	3	4	5	6	7	8	9	10
Needs Improvement				Satisfactory			Outstanding		

Actions for development :

Introducing the Session
____ Provides comfort/warm-up for group
____ Overviews ground rules
____ Places goal/wish/challenge statement on flip chart
____ Reinforces and supports client role
____ Clarifies roles and invites participation
____ Reinforces client's commitment to Goal/Wish/Challenge
____ Numbers and labels pages
____ Uses appropriate transition to next stage

1	2	3	4	5	6	7	8	9	10
Needs Improvement				Satisfactory			Outstanding		

Actions for development :

Assess/Gather Data
____ Lists data on flip chart
____ Numbers and labels pages
____ Asks gather data questions
____ Has resource group write problem statements while client gives data
____ Checks back with client
____ Considers many kinds of data
____ Stretches data appropriately, uses senses
____ Involves resource group
____ Identifies important data to carry forward
____ Prepares transition to Formulate the Challenge stage

1	2	3	4	5	6	7	8	9	10
Needs Improvement				Satisfactory			Outstanding		

Actions for development :

FACILITATION

Formulate the Challenge
____ Numbers and labels pages FC
____ Uses proper statement starters (IWWM, HM, H2, WMBAT)
____ Uses components of problem statement (statement starter, owner, action, verb, goal)
____ Uses stretching techniques appropriately (Asks questions with the the 5Ws; uses Word Dance and "Why? What's Stopping You?")
____ Probes appropriately
____ Checks back with client
____ Encourages resource group participation
____ Converges on problem statement (highlighting)
____ Checks commitment of problem statement for Explore Ideas
____ Uses appropriate transition to next stage

1	2	3	4	5	6	7	8	9	10
Needs Improvement				Satisfactory			Outstanding		

Actions for development :

Explore Ideas
____ Numbers and labels pages EI
____ Sets quota or idea goal (30-40)
____ Involves resource group
____ Encourages builds
____ Probes when appropriate
____ Checks back with client
____ Uses appropriate stretching techniques
____ Selects most promising ideas (highlighting)
____ Prepares for Formulate Solutions
____ Uses appropriate transition to next stage

1	2	3	4	5	6	7	8	9	10
Needs Improvement				Satisfactory			Outstanding		

Actions for development :

FACILITATION

Formulate Solutions
____ Numbers and labels pages FS
____ Uses appropriate strategy (Praise First; Evaluation Matrix; Card Sort; Targeting)
____ Determines strengths and weakness of ideas
____ Checks back with client
____ Involves resource group appropriately
____ Prepares for the next stage
____ Uses appropriate transition to next stage

```
1     2     3     4     5     6     7     8     9     10
  Needs Improvement       Satisfactory         Outstanding
```

Actions for development :

Explore Acceptance
____ Numbers and labels pages EA
____ Identifies sources of assistance/resistance
____ Overcomes resistance
____ Checks with client
____ Involves resource group appropriately

Plan for Action
____ Numbers and labels pages PFA
____ Determines action
____ Develops plan (what will be done, by whom, by when, reporting completion to whom)
____ Checks client commitment to plan
____ Provides appropriate closure to session

```
1     2     3     4     5     6     7     8     9     10
  Needs Improvement       Satisfactory         Outstanding
```

Actions for development :

FACILITATION

Client Interview Worksheet

Based on your client interview, complete the information below.
Attach extra pages as needed, especially for "data."

Client: _____
Date: _____
Area of Concern (initial goal, wish, challenge): IWBGI.... I wish... _____
_____
_____

Data

What is a brief history of the situation?
Who is involved in the situation?
Who is the decision maker?
How do you own this challenge?
Who needs to be a part of the solution?
Who might gain if the situation is resolved?
What successes have you achieved so far?
What are things that have helped you?
What are some obstacles you've encountered?
Where have you found help? Obstacles?

When is the situation occurring or reoccurring?
When would you like to have action taken?
How long has this been a concern?
Why is it a concern for you?
Why might this be an opportunity for you?
What's been thought of or tried already?
What are your gut feelings about this challenge?
How are your feelings affecting your behavior?
What might be your ideal outcome or goal?
What else?

Initial problem statement(s): H2... HM... IWWM... WMBAT... _____
_____
_____

Purpose and desired outcomes of upcoming session: _____
_____
_____

Session Plan

CPS Stage: _____
Statement (w/starter): _____
Initial tool selection: _____
Session date: _____
Time: From _____ To _____
Location: _____
Logistical needs: _____

Resource group members: _____
_____

Who will begin session? _____
How? _____

General notes:

© 2011 Miller, Vehar, Firestien, Thurber, Nielsen

Statement of the challenge:

Brainwriting Worksheet

Row 1

Row 2

Row 3

F-88

© 2011 Miller, Vehar, Firestien, Thurber, Nielsen

FACILITATION

Idea Box Worksheet

Statement of the challenge:

Write your statement of the challenge in the space above. Then, create column headings that describe the main characteristics or attributes of the challenge. Fill in each column with various options.

Characteristics ☞

Options ☞

The Idea Box is based on the "Morphological Matrix." Read more in Discovery, Invention, Research through the Morphological Approach. *Zwicky, Fritz* (1969). The Macmillan Company.

© 2011 Miller, Vehar, Firestien, Thurber, Nielsen

FACILITATION

Visual Acuity

Pictures perfect for Visual Connections

Visual Connections is a great tool for getting groups to branch out in their creative thinking. But you need great pictures to get great ideas. Finding images that trigger creative thoughts is trickier than you might think! Not every great picture is a great Visual Connections picture. Here are some tips to help you choose the best.

Go for pictures in the following general categories:
1.) **People (alone or interacting)**
2.) **Animals**
3.) **Nature/Landscape**
4.) **Food**
5.) **Machinery**

Avoid: Photos of recognizable or controversial figures, highly charged photos, including those of illness, death or erotic subjects.

Hint:
Mix it up. For example, if your client is working on a challenge that involves machinery, pick images of people, food, landscapes or animals. If your client is brainstorming on new pasta varieties, show picture of machines, nature, etc.

Visual Connections Worksheet

What do you see? What do you feel like? What would it be like if you were here? What memories have you had like this? What experiences have you had like this? What might this taste/sound/smell/feel like?

Object #1

Your observations from the stimulus

a)_____
b) _____
c)_____
d) _____

Connections to the problem statement

a) _____
b) _____
c)_____
d) _____

Object #2

Your observations from the stimulus

a)_____
b) _____
c)_____
d) _____

Connections to the problem statement

a) _____
b) _____
c)_____
d) _____

Object #3

Your observations from the stimulus

a)_____
b) _____
c)_____
d) _____

Connections to the problem statement

a) _____
b) _____
c)_____
d) _____

Statement of the challenge:

FACILITATION

Evaluation Matrix Worksheet

Rating scale: Excellent Okay Poor
                  A B C D E

Options / Criteria

Sidney Parnes uses the evaluation matrix in his Creative Behavior Guidebook and Creative Behavior Workbook.

Praise First Worksheet

If you have generated ideas and narrowed them down to a few promising options, here's your chance to strengthen, improve, and craft them into workable solutions. Begin by writing your most promising option in the form of an "action statement," beginning with the statement starter "What I see myself (us) doing is..." This statement should include a specific, measurable result. The measure can be as stringent as metrics or dollars, or as simple as verifying that you have accomplished the solution. Write your action statement below.

ACTION STATEMENT
What I see myself (us) doing is:

Wait!!! Do not fill in the following chart until you have completed the next three pages.

In order to:	Do this:
In order to:	Do this:
In order to:	Do this:
In order to:	Do this:
In order to:	Do this:

© 2011 Miller, Vehar, Firestien, Thurber, Nielsen

FACILITATION

Praise First

Now, run a Praise First or POINt evaluation on your action statement. Remember, POINt stands for Pluses, Opportunities, Issues and New thinking. The idea is to articulate what's good about the idea, then to consider and overcome any concerns you have.

Below list at least three **pluses** or specific strengths of your idea.

1.

2.

3.

Now, list at least three **opportunities,** speculations, spin-offs or possible future gains that could result from your idea. In a future when this idea has become a reality, what has become possible? List potentials, using the statement starter "It might..."

1. *It might:*

2. *It might:*

3. *It might:*

Finally, list any **issues** you have with the idea. Be sure to phrase each issue as an open-ended question that will allow you to overcome each one and move forward.

1. *How to:*

2. *How to:*

3. *How to:*

FACILITATION

Review your issues. Decide which are most important. List your most important issue below and generate at least 15 ways to overcome it. Once you have enough ideas to overcome that issue, go to your next most important issue and generate ways to overcome it. Do this until all of your issues have been overcome. Remember, the ground rules for brainstorming are very important in helping you to find ways to overcome your concerns.

Issue #1) How to...
Ideas for overcoming issue #1:

1. 9.
2. 10.
3. 11.
4. 12.
5. 13.
6. 14.
7. 15.
8.

Issue #2) How to...
Ideas for overcoming issue #2:

1. 9.
2. 10.
3. 11.
4. 12.
5. 13.
6. 14.
7. 15.
8.

Issue #3) How to...
Ideas for overcoming issue #3:

1. 9.
2. 10.
3. 11.
4. 12.
5. 13.
6. 14.
7. 15.
8.

© 2011 Miller, Vehar, Firestien, Thurber, Nielsen

FACILITATION

Issue #4) How to...
Ideas for overcoming issue #4:

1.
2.
3.
4.
5.
6.
7.
8.

9.
10.
11.
12.
13.
14.
15.

Issue #5) How to...
Ideas for overcoming issue #5:

1.
2.
3.
4.
5.
6.
7.
8.

9.
10.
11.
12.
13.
14.
15.

Put a check mark by the best ideas for overcoming each issue.
Then, turn back to page one of this worksheet. Phrase each issue as a statement using the statement starter "In order to..." and include your best ideas.

For example, an issue over funding might start as:
"How might I get funding?"

After brainstorming, you might end up filling in page one by writing:
"In order to obtain funding, we will petition the division vice president and prove a cost-reduction over the next 18 months."

PPCO is a creativity tool developed by Multiple Resource Associates.

Action Plan Worksheet

Now, looking at the new and improved action statement, refine your solution even further.

Action Planning Questions

Below are a number of questions designed to help you gain acceptance for your solution and prepare for action by helping you identify assisters and resisters. Take a moment to answer each question.

- *What might I do to gain acceptance of my idea?*

- *What might I do to gain enthusiasm for my idea?*

- *How might I insure the effectiveness of my idea?*

- *What additional resources might help me implement my idea*

  (individuals, groups, materials, money)?

- *How might I pretest my idea?*

- *What special times might I use (day, week, month, year)?*

- *What special places or locations might I use?*

Using a flipchart, whiteboard, post-its or just a pad of paper, brainstorm all the possible action steps you could take to make your action statement a reality. (Include your responses to the action planning questions above.) Then converge: select all the action steps that will help you reach your goal and use them to fill in the Plan for Action chart on the next page.

Hint: Be sure to make one of your first steps something you can accomplish within the next 24 hours. Momentum is essential in the creative process!

Plan for Action

Action	by whom?	by when?	reporting completion to whom?
short-term			
mid-term			
long-term			

PPCO is a creativity tool developed by Multiple Resource Associates. This version of Creative Problem Solving developed by Miller and Vehar (1994), Firestien (1995). Adapted from Osborn (1953), Parnes, Noller and Biondi (1977), Firestien (1989), Isaksen, Dorval and Treffinger (1994).

Targeting worksheet

The bull's-eye:
In the space below, describe your ideal state: Use pictures, words, and other visuals to bring your ideal state to life.

Where are you now?
Place the dart (option; what I see myself doing is…) on the target in relation to your ideal state.

Why are you off center?
Explain the forces that pull the idea toward the center (i.e. why it's good) and the forces that push it away (why it's not exactly on target).

Pulls   ·   Pushes

What would help get you to the bull's-eye?
Turn pushes into "How to…" statements and brainstorm ideas.

How to…   Ideas:

How to…   Ideas:

How to…   Ideas:

Ready, Set, Go!
Pick the ideas that will help turn pushes into pulls and write a new action statement using the statement starter…What I now see myself doing is…

TERMS

Bull's-eye: Your ideal/future state
Dart: The best option(s) you are considering
Pull: Positive force that pulls the option towards the bull's-eye
Push: Negative force that pushes the option away from the bulls-eye

© 2011 Miller, Vehar, Firestien, Thurber, Nielsen

FACILITATION

The Idea Seizer

Carpe idea

Friends, Romans, resource group members...

Once the ideas have been generated and highlighted, pick the one that "grabs" you. It can be an idea that others have already highlighted or a stray idea that escaped notice. Use this full page to elaborate on the idea.

Product Concept Worksheet

Picture this....

Who is the product for?
What needs does it meet?

What is the product like?
Describe the primary qualities of the product. Think about form and function, such as appearance, shape, size, portions, smell, texture, ingredients, packaging.

What does this product offer the user?
Think about sensory, functional, physical and emotional benefits to the user.

What does your product look like?
Sketch it, or illustrate its features on the back of this sheet.

© 2011 Miller, Vehar, Firestien, Thurber, Nielsen

FACILITATION

To Learn More

Key Bibliography
To learn more about Creative Problem Solving facilitation, we recommend the following sources:

Books

Eckert, R., Vehar, J. (2007). *More Lightning Less Thunder: How to energize innovation teams.* New Palz, NY: New & Improved, LLC.

Firestien, R.L. (1998). *Why didn't I think of that? A personal and professional guide to better ideas and decision making.* Williamsville, NY: Innovation Resources, Inc.

Firestien, R.L. (1996). *Leading on the Creative Edge: Gaining competitive advantage through the power of Creative Problem Solving.* Colorado Springs, CO: Piñon Press.

Hartmann, K. and Nielsen, D. (2011). *Inspired: How creative people think, work and find inspiration.* Amsterdam: BIS Publishers.

May, R. (1976). *The Courage to Create.* New York, NY: Bantam.

Miller, B., Vehar, J., Firestien, R., Thurber, S., Nielsen, D., (2011) *Creativity Unbound: An introduction to creative process.* Evanston, IL: FourSight, LLC.

Osborn, A.F. (1993). *Applied Imagination.* Buffalo, NY: Creative Education Foundation.

Parnes, S.J. (1997). *Optimize the Magic of Your Mind.* Buffalo, NY: Creative Education Foundation in association with Bearly Limited.

Parnes, S.J. (1985). *A facilitating style of leadership.* Buffalo, NY: Creative Education Foundation.

Parnes, S.J. (1988). *Visionizing.* Buffalo, NY: Creative Education Foundation.

Puccio, G., Mance, M., Murdock, M. (2011) *Creative Leadership.* Thousand Oaks, CA: Sage.

Ray, M. and Myers, R. (1986). *Creativity in Business.* Garden City, NY: Doubleday.

Rohnke, K. (1984). *Silver Bullets.* Dubuque, IA: Kendall/Hunt.

Shekerjian, D. (1990). *Uncommon Genius.* New York, NY: Viking Penguin.

Schwarz, R. (2002). *The Skilled Facilitator.* San Francisco, CA: Jossey-Bass.

VanGundy, A.B. (1992). *Idea Power: Techniques and Resources to Unleash the Creativity in Your Organization.* New York, NY: AMACOM.

Websites
www.blairmiller.com
www.buffalostate.edu/centers/creativity
www.foursightonline.com
www.newandimproved.com
www.RogerFirestien.com

Assessments
FourSight: The Breakthrough Thinking Profile is available for purchase on the web at www.foursightonline.com.

Audiotapes

Firestien, R.L. (1987, 1989, 1996). *Power Think: Achieving Your Goals Through Mental Rehearsal.* Williamsville, NY: Innovation Resources, Inc.

Firestien, R.L. (1993). *Breakthrough: Getting Better Ideas.* Williamsville, NY: Innovation Resources, Inc.

Firestien, R.L. (1988). *From Basics to Breakthroughs: A guide to better thinking and decision making.* Williamsville, NY: Innovation Resources, Inc.

Videotapes

Firestien, R.L. (1998). *Roger Firestien Speaks! Leading On The Creative Edge: Spotlight Presentation at the 43rd Annual Creative Problem Solving Institute Conference.* Chicago, IL: Zepcom and the Creative Education Foundation.

Firestien, R.L., Vehar, J.R., Chamberlain, S. (1998). *Applying Creativity Video Series* (12 videos). Buffalo, NY: Innovation Resources, Inc. and the Creative Education Foundation.

Firestien, R.L. (1994). *Unleashing the Power of Creativity: The key to teamwork, empowerment, and continuous improvement.* Buffalo, NY: Kinetic Films, Inc.

Roger Firestien's materials are available through Innovation Resources, Inc., P.O. Box 615 Williamsville, NY 14231, Tel: (716) 631-3564

References

Key Reference List

Amabile, Teresa, et. al. (1995) *KEYS: User's Guide*. Greensboro, NC.: Center for Creative Leadership.

Avarello, L.L., Coleman, S.E., Miller, B.J., Puccio, G.J., & Vehar, J.R. (1994). *CPS in action*. Chicago: Blair J. Miller.

Battelle-Institut. (1972) *Methoden und organization der ideenfindung in der industrie (Methods and organization of idea finding in industry)*. Frankfurt, Germany: Battelle.

Butler, R.J. (1981). Innovation in organizations: Appropriateness of perspectives from small group studies for strategy formulation. *Human Resources, 34(9)*, 763-788.

Creative Thinking and Creative Problem Solving. (1994). Buffalo, NY: Creative Education Foundation.

Eberle, R. F. (1971) *Scamper: Games for imagination development*. Buffalo, NY: DOK.

Ekvall, G. (1983). *Climate, structure and innovativeness of organizations: A theoretical framework and an experiment*. Stockholm, Sweden: The Swedish Council for Management and Organizational Behaviour.

Firestien, R.L and Vehar, J.R. (1997). *Insights into innovation*. Buffalo, NY: Roger L. Firestien, Ph.D.

Firestien, R.L. (1996). *Leading on the creative edge*. Colorado Springs, CO: Pinon Press.

Firestien, R.L. (1988). *From basics to breakthroughs: A guide to better thinking and decision-making*. Williamsville, NY: Innovation Resources, Inc.

Firestien, R. L. (1983). Ownership and converging: Essential ingredients of Creative Problem Solving. *Journal of Creative Behavior, 17(1)*, 32-38.

Firestien, R.L., & Treffinger, D.J. (1989, November/December). Update: Guidelines for effective facilitation of creative problem solving (part 2). *Gifted Child Today*, 40-44.

Firestien, R.L., & Treffinger, D.J. (1989, September/October). Update: Guidelines for effective facilitation of creative problem solving (part 3). *Gifted Child Today*, 44-47.

Gardner, J.W. (1990). *On leadership*. New York: Free Press.

Geschka, H. (1979). *Methods and organization of idea generation*. Creativity Week Two, 1979 Proceedings. Greensboro, N.C: Center for Creative Leadership.

Gordon, W. (1961). *Synectics*. New York: Harper & Row.

Hayakawa, S.I. (1978). *Language in thought and action*, fourth edition. New York: Harcourt Brace Jovanovich.

Heider, J. (1985). *The tao of leadership: Lao Tzu's tao te ching adapted for a new age*. Atlanta, GA: Humanics New Age.

Isaksen, S.G. (1983). Toward a model for the facilitation of creative problem solving. *Journal of Creative Behavior, 17(1)*, 18-31.

Isaksen, S. G., Dorval, K. B., & Treffinger, D. J. (1994). *Creative approaches to problem solving*. Dubuque, IA.: Kendall/Hunt Publishing Company.

Isaksen, S.G. & Treffinger, D.J. (1985). *Creative Problem Solving: The basic course*. Buffalo, NY: Bearly Limited.

Korzybski, A. (1933). *Science and sanity, an introduction to non-Aristotelin systems and general semantics*. (publisher unknown).

Michalko, M. (1991). *Thinkertoys*. Berkeley, CA: Ten Speed.

Miller, B.J. (1992). *The use of outdoor-based training initiatives to enhance the understanding of creative problem solving*, Buffalo, NY: Center for Studies in Creativity.

Osborn, A. F. (1953). *Applied imagination: Principles and procedures of Creative Problem Solving*. New York: Scribner's.

Osborn, A. F. (1993). *Applied imagination: Principles and procedures of Creative Problem Solving* (3rd ed.). Buffalo, NY: The Creative Education Foundation Press.

Parnes, S.J. (1988). *Visionizing*. Buffalo, NY: Creative Education Foundation.

Parnes, S.J. (1985). *A facilitating style of leadership*. Buffalo, NY: Bearly Limited.

Parnes, S.J. (1981). *The magic of your mind*. Buffalo, NY: The Creative Education Foundation.

Parnes, S.J. (1967). *Creative behavior guidebook*. New York: Charles Scribner's Sons.

Parnes, S.J. (1967). *Creative behavior workbook*. New York: Charles Scribner's Sons.

Parnes, S.J. *Creative leadership*. Unpublished manuscript.

Rhodes, M. (1961). An analysis of creativity. *Phi Delta Kappa, 42*, 305-310.

Rowe, Mary Budd. (Spring 1987). Wait time: Slowing down may be a way of speeding up. *American Educator 11*: 38-43, 47.

Shaw, M.E. (1976). *The personal environment of groups. Group dynamics: The psychology of small group behavior* (2nd ed.) New York: McGraw-Hill.

Treffinger, D.J., & Firestien, R.L. (1989 July/August). Guidelines for effective facilitation of creative problem solving (part 1). *Gifted Child Today*, 35-39.

Treffinger, D.J. & Firestien, R.L. (1983). Ownership and converging: Essential ingredients of Creative Problem Solving. *Journal of Creative Behavior, 17(1)*, 32-38.

Treffinger, D.J., Isaksen, S.G. & Firestien, R.L. (1983). Theoretical perspectives on creative learning and its facilitation: An overview. *Journal of Creative Behavior, 17(1)*, 9-17.

Treffinger, D.J., Isaksen, S.G. & Firestien, R.L. (1982). *Handbook for creative learning (vol. 1)*. Williamsville, NY: Center for Creative Learning.

Tuckman, B.W. (1965). Developmental sequence in small groups. *Psychological Bulletin, 63(6)*, 384-399.

Vehar, J.R., Shephard, W.J., Brese, C.A. (1995). *The art of CPS facilitation*. Buffalo, NY: Creative Education Foundation.

Vehar, J.R, Lunken, H.P., Brese, C.A., & Shephard, W.J. (1995). *The art of facilitation*. Buffalo, NY: Creative Education Foundation.

Vehar, J.R. (1994). *CPS toolbook for group facilitators*. (Unpublished manuscript available from Jonathan Vehar, New & Improved, P.O. Box 7043, Santa Monica, California 90406.)

FACILITATION

Notes: